WHERE LOVE Begins

LISA RENÉE RUGGERI

Disclaimer:
This is a work of fiction. Names, characters, businesses, places, events, and incidents are either the products of the author's imagination or used in a fictitious manner. Any resemblance to actual persons, living or dead, or actual events is purely coincidental.

ISBN: 979-8308911418

For Maria.
Gone too soon but never forgotten...

Prologue

The convent was cloaked in an eerie stillness, broken only by the soft shuffle of Sister Augusta's footsteps. She walked the narrow, dimly lit hallway toward the nursery, where a small bundle lay waiting—Isabella's son. His cries were faint now, as though sensing the inevitable separation that loomed ahead. Sister Augusta paused at the door, her heart heavy with the weight of what was about to transpire.

In 1966, the world outside the convent was moving fast—protests, revolutions, the rise of new freedoms—but within these walls, time stood still, locked in the rhythm of prayer and sacrifice. Sister Augusta had always believed in the sanctity of her vows, in doing what was right for the children who passed through these hallowed halls. But today, doubt ate at her conscience.

The couple waiting in the sitting room were impatient. They'd been vetted, of course—well off, polished, the kind of parents who could provide a life Isabella never could. Still, as Sister Augusta cradled the infant in her arms, she hesitated at the doorway.

The woman—elegant in her fur-trimmed coat—turned, her face cold but beautiful. The man rose to his feet, impatience flickering in his steely blue eyes. "We'll take him now," the woman said sharply, "but we want the file as well."

Sister Augusta's hands trembled. "The file?" she repeated, her voice barely a whisper.

"Yes," the man replied, his voice clipped. "We want it destroyed. Permanently. No trace left behind."

"But the records—" Sister Augusta began, unsure.

The woman's eyes narrowed, and she reached into her coat, pulling out a thick envelope. "This should cover it. We trust you'll do what's necessary."

The envelope, heavy with bills, was thrust into the nun's hands. A donation, they called it. A bribe, it felt like. Sister Augusta stared at it, torn between duty and the unspoken truth that lay behind the couple's request. It wasn't about the money—it was about erasing this child's history, ensuring he would never be found. But what if Isabella changed her mind? What if one day she wanted her son back?

Her body pulsated as she retrieved the file from her desk. The crinkling of the paper was loud in the suffocating silence of the parlor. She held it tightly, as if the file itself held more than just records—it held a child's identity, a mother's hope. Slowly, almost reluctantly, she handed it over.

The woman snatched the file from her hands with a smile that didn't reach her eyes. "Good," she said. "This chapter is closed."

As the couple left the convent, Sister Augusta watched them from the narrow window. Something gnawed at her, a deep-rooted unease that she couldn't shake. Isabella had trusted her with the most precious thing in her life, and now that trust felt like it had been shattered. A cold wind blew through the gap in the window, chilling her to the bone.

Without a second thought, she threw on her cloak and hurried outside. The couple's car was already pulling away, and in a flash of desperation, she flagged down a yellow cab. "Follow that car," she instructed the driver, her heart pounding in her chest.

The drive seemed endless, every turn deepening her dread. They left the city behind, winding into the quiet, sleepy streets of a small town in upstate New York. Finally, the couple's car pulled up to a large, stately home. Sister Augusta watched from a distance, memorizing every detail—the large oak tree by the driveway, the stone pathway leading to the front door. She scribbled the address on a small scrap of paper and clutched it tightly.

As the cab pulled away to take her back to the convent, the wind picked up. Sister Augusta didn't notice at first—she was lost in her thoughts—but the paper, the one with the address, slipped from her pocket. It tumbled out as she left the cab, caught in the gust, and was gone before she could react.

Panic surged through her. She told herself it didn't matter—she had the house etched in her memory. But memory is a fragile thing, and as the years passed, even the sharpest memories could dull, blur, or fade entirely.

And one day, when Isabella would come looking, would she remember?

The wind howled louder as the cab sped down the empty highway, leaving behind only questions and shadows of what was to come...

Two years had passed since the storm of revelations shattered Angela's world. The secrets, the lies, and the truth about her mother and father had weighed heavily on her mind, but time, as always, found a way to heal—or at least patch up—the wounds. Angela had settled into her life in New York City, and now, things seemed to be falling into place.

The city bustled around her as she walked hand in hand with Jay down a leafy path in Central Park. The crisp autumn air nipped at their cheeks, and the golden leaves crunched underfoot. New York had a way of wrapping them in its vibrant pulse, a comforting rhythm they had grown used to. They had their routines now—afternoon walks through the park, brunches at a little café in the Village, lazy evenings watching the sun dip below the skyline. It was an almost surreal happiness, a calm after the storm.

Angela was in her second year of college, finally at the same school as Jay. They had created a little bubble together, surrounded by friends, love, and a sense of normalcy. But normal was a strange word to Angela now. How could anything feel normal after the whirlwind of family drama and dark secrets that had come to light? She shook off the thoughts as Jay squeezed her hand gently, pulling her back into the present.

"You good?" he asked, his brown eyes warm with concern.

Angela smiled up at him, her heart swelling with affection. "Yeah, I'm good," she said softly, her voice barely louder than the rustle of leaves in the wind. And for the most part, she was. They had been through so much, but together, they had come out stronger.

Life had even found a way to restore some semblance of family. Angela and her father, Daniel, had begun to mend their broken relationship. Most Sundays, they gathered for dinner—Daniel, his new wife Susie, baby Joshua and Jay. It was strange at first, seeing her father so different from the cold, distant man she had grown up with. Now, with Joshua, his son and Angela's half-brother, Daniel seemed softer. He laughed more, loved more, and though the scars of the past hadn't fully healed, he was trying. And Angela appreciated that.

She could still picture the day of Daniel and Susie's wedding. It had been a small, intimate affair in the Hamptons. Angela had stood as a bridesmaid, wearing a soft pink dress that fluttered in the wind. Jay had been the best man, of course, standing tall, handsome and proud next to Daniel. Little Joshua had toddled down the aisle as the page boy, his tiny face beaming with joy. But there had been an absence, one Angela couldn't ignore. Her sisters—Francesca, Bianca, and Camilla—had refused to come. They hadn't forgiven Daniel for what they called his "betrayal," abandoning their mother for a small-town woman with a child born out of wedlock. In their world, reputation was everything.

As the memories flitted through her mind, Angela glanced up at Jay. He was talking about something—a new class, or maybe their weekend plans—but she found herself drifting, lost in thoughts of how much had changed, and yet how much still felt unresolved. The past, it seemed, was never fully behind her.

Jay stopped walking, turning to face her with that look of quiet intensity he got when he sensed she was far away.

"What's going on in that head of yours?" he asked, his thumb brushing her cheek.

Angela hesitated, searching for the right words. "It's just...sometimes I think I'm okay, and then I remember everything. My mom, my sisters, my dad...everything that happened. It feels like a lifetime ago, but at the same time, it's like it all just happened yesterday."

Jay wrapped his arms around her, pulling her close. "You don't have to go through it alone, you know. I'm here. Always."

Angela closed her eyes, letting herself melt into his embrace. He was her anchor, her safe place. And yet, there was still an unsettled feeling deep inside her. As if the past wasn't quite done with her yet.

Every morning, Angela woke up to the sound of bustling streets below her apartment window, the soft sunlight filtering through the curtains. The city, with all its noise and energy, had become her sanctuary. She found peace in the pattern of her routine, a stark contrast to the isolation she had once felt in her family's cold penthouse.

Jay was in his third year of economics and finance, a far cry from his original dream of becoming a teacher. He'd always had a passion for mentoring, for guiding others. But Daniel had a way of influencing people. He had persuaded Jay to switch to a course that would prepare him to join the Hastings empire, an empire built on wealth, connections, and endless influence. Angela saw it happening, the subtle way Daniel was molding Jay into his protégé, but she wasn't sure how Jay felt about it. He never complained, but there was a quiet shift in him, a shadow of doubt that sometimes flickered behind his brown eyes.

Angela, however, was exactly where she wanted to be. Studying to be a vet had always been her dream. It was her way of caring, of giving love in a world that had often been so cold and unkind to her. Her classes at college were intense but rewarding, and she thrived in the hands-on environment. The scent of antiseptic and the steady hum of the clinic filled her senses during practicals, and she found a strange peace in it all. Animals, at least, couldn't lie or manipulate—they were pure, and her connection to them was instinctive.

Just as the new semester began, a fresh face appeared on campus—a new professor who sparked curiosity inside of Angela. His name was Michael Fitzpatrick, a man whose energy radiated through every lecture he gave. He wasn't like the other professors, staid and detached; he was passionate, vibrant, and had a deep love for veterinary science that Angela found infectious. His enthusiasm was like a spark, igniting something in her she hadn't felt in a long time—a true belief in herself.

Professor Fitzpatrick saw potential in Angela from the moment she walked into his class. She stood out, not just because of her academic dedication but because of her kindness, her care, and her quiet determination. He often singled her out during lectures, asking her to share her thoughts and pushing her to question more, dig deeper. "You've got what it takes to be great," he told her one afternoon after class, his eyes bright with conviction. "Don't ever let anyone tell you otherwise."

Angela thrived under his mentorship, pouring herself into her studies with a passion that sometimes surprised even her. It wasn't just about getting the grades; she wanted to make a difference. She wanted to be the kind of vet that made a real impact, and under Mr Fitzpatrick's guidance, she felt like she was on her way.

Her life wasn't just school and study, though. Living in New York meant she was surrounded by friends and the vibrant energy of the city. Her best friend, Sophie, had moved up a few months ago, and Angela couldn't have been happier. Sophie had been another light in her life during the past few years, and now they got to share the city together. Sophie had dreams of becoming a chef, and she was determined to land an apprenticeship with one of the top restaurants in New York. They often spent evenings in Sophie's tiny apartment, experimenting with new recipes or visiting the latest hot spot in the culinary scene, laughing over delicacies and dreams for the future.

Angela and Jay had introduced Sophie to their circle of college friends, who welcomed her with open arms. Their group was tight-knit, always up for an adventure, whether it was a spontaneous night out in the city or long, late-night talks over coffee. But no matter how much fun they had in the city, they never forgot where they came from.

At least once a month, they'd pile into Jay's old car and head back to the coast to spend a weekend with their old friends—Liam, Maddie, and Derek. There was something comforting about returning to the familiar. The wind was always colder by the beach, and the air had that salty, briny taste that made Angela feel alive. Even in the freezing cold, they'd strip off their shoes and splash in the ocean, laughing

15

as the icy waves crashed against their legs. They'd build bonfires on the beach, the flames crackling as they huddled close, reminiscing about old times and making plans for the future. The stars above them felt bigger out there, away from the city lights, and sometimes, as Angela looked up, she'd feel a deep sense of peace.

Angela was content to live in the moment, to savor the happiness she had worked so hard to find. But as she stood on the beach with Jay's arms wrapped around her, the salty wind in her hair, she couldn't shake the feeling that something was about to change. Something big.

On a warm October Saturday, Angela and Jay sat around a blazing bonfire on the beach, the glow of the flames dancing across their faces. The air was crisp, the kind of evening that hinted at the end of autumn, but the fire kept them all warm as they huddled together with their friends. They were laughing, talking, and throwing out ideas for the upcoming millennium celebrations. The turn of the year 2000 was approaching fast, and everyone was buzzing with excitement about how to make the night unforgettable.

"So, what are we going to do?" Jay asked, breaking the comfortable silence that had settled over them. He leaned back on his elbows, gazing at Angela with a playful grin. "It's got to be epic, right? This is once in a lifetime stuff."

Angela smiled at him and looked around at the rest of their group, the gang that had become like her second family. "Bianca's hosting a big party," she said, rolling her eyes. "You know, one of those super fancy, formal things. We're trying to get out of it."

The group burst into laughter, knowing there was no way Angela and Jay would be caught dead at one of Bianca's stuffy high-society events, especially not on a night like New Year's Eve. Jay shook his head. "No way, Ella. We have to do something fun. Something that's actually memorable, not just for show."

Angela felt a rush of warmth at how they still called her Ella. It was a name that held so much history for her, a part of her that she'd shared only with them. Jay and his friends had been there through everything, and even now, as her life in the city expanded and she rebuilt her relationship with her father, she never stopped feeling like Ella when she was with them. It was a special connection, a private identity that felt like a secret code between them.

Ideas for the millennium party started flying around the circle. Liam leaned forward; his eyes gleaming with mischief. "How about we rent a boat and sail into the new millennium?"

Derek shook his head, laughing. "And freeze to death on the ocean? No thanks."

Maddie jumped in, her hands waving in the air. "What if we throw a bonfire party—like this, but bigger! With fireworks?"

Jay nodded thoughtfully. "Not bad, but we need more. Something no one will forget."

It was Sophie who came up with the perfect plan. She leaned in, her face lit by the glow of the fire. "I've got it," she said, her voice full of excitement. "Let's have our own huge party at the café! We can decorate it with different decades from the 20th century. Everyone can dress up as their favorite era, and we'll turn it into a massive town event. We'll invite everyone, make it a celebration no one will forget! My parents will totally be on board."

The group erupted into cheers, the excitement was electric. Derek pulled out a notepad and started jotting down ideas as everyone began to brainstorm.

"We could have a '20s jazz corner," suggested Maddie, "with flapper dresses and old-school champagne!"

"And a '50s diner theme with milkshakes and rock 'n' roll!" added Liam.

Jay chuckled, shaking his head. "I'm calling the '80s section. We'll get a DJ and have a dance floor with neon lights and disco balls."

Angela leaned back, listening to her friends' enthusiasm as they sketched out what was sure to be an epic New Year's Eve party. She loved how they were all in this together. The past few years had been filled with challenges, but here on the beach, everything felt so simple, so right. This was the life she had always wanted, full of love, laughter, and a sense of belonging.

But as the conversation flowed around her, Angela's thoughts began to drift back to the dilemma she hadn't quite figured out yet—how to get out of Bianca's party. It wasn't just about dodging another stuffy, high-society gathering. No, it was far more complicated than that. Her sisters hadn't forgiven her for siding with their father after everything that had come to light. To them, it wasn't just about loyalty; it was betrayal, pure and simple. Angela had chosen to maintain a relationship with Daniel when they had all but cut him out of their lives. It had damaged what was once a sisterly bond between them, especially with Bianca. She took it the hardest.

In her sisters' eyes, Angela's decision to stay close to Daniel and, by extension, to Jay and his family, felt like she was turning her back on them and everything they had been through together. They couldn't see it the way Angela did. For her, it wasn't about choosing sides. It was about forging her own path, one that included the people she loved—both old and new. She had tried so many times to explain that to them, to make them understand that she wasn't rejecting them or their pain, but rather embracing the life she was building with Jay.

Angela had grown so close to Jay's family. His mom, Susie, was so warm and welcoming, the kind of maternal figure she'd always craved but never really had. Susie had embraced her like a daughter, treating her with kindness and respect that had made her feel truly seen. Spending time with her was like stepping into a world of comfort she hadn't known before. And then there was Joshua, who had become a bright light in her life. She adored him. Every time she held him, played with him, or saw his innocent smile, Angela felt a deep connection. It was a bond she wanted to nurture, something precious that she refused to let slip away.

But her sisters refused to see that side of things. They couldn't—or wouldn't—understand that Jay's family was part of her life now, and Daniel, as complicated as their history was, was still her father. Angela couldn't just walk away from him, not when he was finally making an effort to be present in her life. And, by extension, she couldn't walk away from Jay or the new life they were building together. Jay and his family were intertwined with her own journey, and that included Daniel, Susie, and Joshua. She wanted to be a part of it all, even if her sisters felt betrayed.

And as much as Angela loved her sisters, their refusal to accept Jay's family had caused a deep rift. They hadn't even given Joshua a chance, a baby who was blameless in the entire situation. They refused to get to know him, refused to acknowledge that he was their brother too. It hurt Angela more than she could say, seeing her sisters draw that line in the sand and cut themselves off from something that could have been a source of joy.

Bianca, in particular, had thrown herself into her high-society life even more, as though the glittering parties and social climbing could shield her from the emotional wreckage left by their father's choices.

Now, with the new millennium approaching, the tension between them felt like a looming storm cloud. Bianca had been planning this extravagant party for months, and Angela knew blowing it off would be another nail in the coffin of their fragile relationship. She could already picture the disappointed look Bianca would give her, the silent judgment from Francesca and Camilla for choosing Jay over her family—again.

Her mother, Isabella, was another challenge altogether. She had become more and more distracted, distant, consumed by her mission to find the son she had given up all those years ago. Conversations with her were strained, every topic overshadowed by Isabella's guilt and regret. No matter how much Angela tried to bring her mother into the present, she couldn't. Isabella was trapped in the past, a prisoner of her own choices, and Angela knew that until she found her son, that would never change.

Angela sighed, glancing at Jay, who caught her eye and smiled. She was so happy here with him, so content in this life they were building. But the weight of her family's discontent still pressed heavily on her. She wanted to move forward, to live in the moment and embrace the future, but Isabella's search for her son hung over them like a shadow.

"Ella, you look worried?" Jay's voice broke into her thoughts.

She nodded, giving him a reassuring smile. "Sorry, I was just thinking about how to break it to my sisters that I won't be going to Bianca's party."

Jay grinned and wrapped his arm around her. "We'll figure it out. This is our night. We'll make it one for the history books."

Angela sighed, watching the flames flicker as her friends' laughter filled the air around her. No matter how much she wanted to smooth things over with her sisters, she couldn't sacrifice her happiness to keep the peace. The millennium was about new beginnings, and maybe, just maybe, this would be the start of her finding a way to bring her two worlds together. But for now, she would focus on the people who made her feel whole, the ones who accepted her as she was, without judgment or strings attached.

Just then, Jay stood up quickly and brushed the sand off his jeans. "I've got to go, guys," he announced, breaking the rhythm of the conversation. "I arranged to meet Daniel back at the house to go over some work stuff."

Angela looked up, concerned. "It's the weekend, Jay. And it's late. Does it really have to be now?"

Jay nodded, his tone firm. "I promised him. There's this big deal coming up, and he wants to show me some paperwork. I don't want to let him down."

Angela's frown deepened. "My father knows this is your final year of college. Surely your studies come first, not his business?"

Jay hesitated, his smile faltering for a brief moment. "I know, Ella, but this deal... it's important. I won't be long, I promise."

Angela sighed, still unconvinced but not wanting to push him further. "Alright, but... you'll come back once you're done, right?"

"It will be late," Jay smiled, leaning down to kiss her on the forehead. "I'll meet you back at the house once you finish up here."

As he walked off into the darkening sky, Angela watched him go, unease building in her chest. Liam, noticing her expression, smirked and called out, "Hey, watch him, Ella—don't let him get all corporate on you!"

The group laughed, but Angela couldn't shake the knot tightening in her stomach as Jay disappeared from sight.

Isabella sat in the center of her sleek, marble penthouse, staring blankly at the glowing screen of her laptop. The pristine view of the New York skyline through the floor-to-ceiling windows couldn't distract her from the words that seemed to mock her: *No leads found.*

She had paid a fortune, sparing no expense in hiring one of the most reputable private investigators in the city. Weeks of waiting for this report had led to nothing but disappointment. Isabella scrolled through the document, her perfectly manicured nails tapping impatiently on the trackpad. The detective had visited the old convent where her son had been given away, but no file had been found. He had interviewed the nuns still remaining, but they had no answers. The most crucial piece—Sister Augusta—wasn't there anymore. And with that, every lead the detective had pursued had dried up, every potential avenue blocked.

But Isabella refused to accept this. No. After everything that had happened—her failed marriage, the cold rejection of her past—there was no way she could let this search end like this. She had to find him.

Closing her laptop with a forceful snap, Isabella leaned back into the plush cushions of the sofa, her mind swirling. She couldn't stop replaying the moment Daniel had confessed that he had never truly loved her. A truth she had known but buried deep within herself, refusing to admit it until it was too late. Her life had been a series of carefully constructed lies. Marrying a man for the sake of stability and acceptance, keeping up appearances in high society, all while denying the hollow emptiness that consumed her.

Her heart had been closed off for years—shut down from love, from connection—ever since that fateful day she had given up her son. She told herself it was necessary, that it had been for the best, but now she knew the truth. That decision had stolen her future, robbed her of the love she could have had with him, with her daughters, and most painfully, with Angela, who had always craved her affection the most.

If I could just find him, she thought desperately. *If I could ask for his forgiveness, maybe I could open my heart again. Maybe I could finally heal.*

Isabella's chest tightened as the longing overwhelmed her. She couldn't allow this detective's dead-end report to be the final word. She knew she had to take matters into her own hands. She needed to find her son herself. There was no other way.

Without hesitation, she reached for her phone, her fingers trembling slightly as she dialed her driver's number.

"Louis, I need you to pick me up immediately," she said, her voice steady but urgent. "We're going to the outskirts of the city. There's a small convent called St. Nicholas'."

She hung up before he could respond, standing up and moving quickly to gather her things. As she grabbed her coat and keys, Isabella glanced around the penthouse—the symbol of a life of wealth and privilege that had brought her everything except happiness. None of this mattered. Not anymore. Her real life, her real purpose, lay somewhere out there—waiting for her, hidden in the shadows of her past.

And now, she was finally ready to face it.

With one last look at the glowing cityscape outside her window, she stepped into the elevator, her heels clicking sharply against the polished floor. The door slid shut, sealing her fate. This was something she had to do herself and there was no turning back now.

Angela arrived home late, her footsteps soft against the hardwood floors as she quietly made her way through the dimly lit house. The faint murmur of voices led her toward her father's study, where she could see Jay and Daniel deep in conversation, papers spread out across the polished oak desk. They were so engrossed in their work that Angela didn't want to disturb them, so she turned and headed to the kitchen instead. .

She found Susie there, tidying up the last remnants of dinner. The soft glow of the kitchen lights cast a warm hue over the room, making it feel cozy and calm, but Angela could sense the lingering tension in the air.

"Not asleep yet?" Angela commented lightly, stepping up beside Susie and taking a clean dish from the rack to dry.

Susie smiled warmly but looked a little tired. "Just waiting for the boys to finish up, then I'll head to bed." She turned toward Angela, her gaze softening. "Are you okay, darling?"

Angela hesitated, leaning against the counter as she considered her words. "I'm just... worried about Jay," she admitted, her voice quiet. "Between working for my father and trying to finish his degree, I'm scared it's all going to be too much for him. I don't want him burning out."

Susie wiped her hands on a dish towel and sighed softly. "I understand your concern, but Jay's excited about this opportunity. You know, he hasn't had much his whole life." She paused, her eyes drifting toward the study door. "Remember, Angela—he spent most of his childhood sleeping on a sofa. This is his chance to make something of himself."

Angela sighed, her fingers fidgeting with the dish in her hands. "I know, I just... I don't want him to work too hard." The thought weighed heavily on her, the idea of Jay being consumed by work the way Daniel had been during her childhood.

Susie turned to face her fully, her expression gentle but firm. "Daniel's a changed man, Angela. He's really trying. He's had the burden of the Hastings empire thrust upon him since he was young- he didn't really have a choice. He's trying to make it work, and at the same time, he's doing his best to be here for us. He's learned from his mistakes—how he wasn't a good father to you and your sisters. He doesn't want to make that mistake again, especially with Joshua."

Angela nodded, though her worry didn't fully dissolve. She set the dish down and folded her arms across her chest.

"I've seen what the family business has done to my family," she said quietly. "I don't want that to happen to Jay."

Susie stepped closer, placing a reassuring hand on her arm. "Jay is different. He's not going to lose himself in all of this. Trust me, he knows what he's doing. And besides," she smiled gently, "Daniel doesn't want to burden him. He wants to share this—make it something they can do together, something that'll bring them closer. That's always been Daniel's dream, to work alongside someone from the family. He's been so desperately unhappy for most of his life, Angela. Work was his escape, but now... he wants to enjoy life- not work so hard. He's trying to do things right this time."

Angela nodded again, though a knot still twisted in her stomach. She wanted to believe it. She wanted to trust that Jay wouldn't get swallowed up by the weight of her father's legacy. But the shadows of her past, of the cold, distant father who had been absent for so much of her childhood, still loomed large.

Before she could say anything more, the door to the study creaked open, and Daniel and Jay stepped out, still discussing whatever paperwork they had been going over. Daniel smiled warmly at his daughter as he walked over and kissed her on the forehead.

"You know, Angela, Jay's incredible with contracts and negotiations. He has a real knack for this," Daniel said, beaming with pride.

Angela forced a smile, though the unease lingered beneath it. "That's great, Father."

Jay came over, wrapping his arms around her from behind, resting his chin on her shoulder. "Sorry I left the group earlier," he murmured into her ear. "I'll make it up to you tomorrow. How about a bike ride along the ocean? Just the two of us."

Angela leaned back into him, her body softening at his touch. "That sounds perfect," she whispered, though her mind still lingered on the conversation in the kitchen.

As they said their goodnights and made their way upstairs to bed, Angela couldn't help but steal a glance at her father. He seemed different now, more present, more engaged in their lives. But the memory of what his work had cost him, and what it had cost their family, still haunted her. She didn't want to lose Jay to the same fate.

Liam's teasing words from earlier echoed in her mind: *Watch him—don't let him get all corporate on you.*

Angela smiled at the thought, but deep down, she knew this was something she would have to keep an eye on.

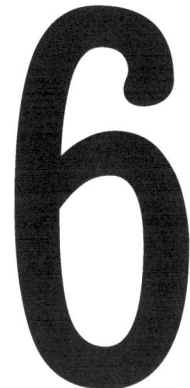

The sun peeked through the trees as Angela and Jay set off on their bike ride, the crisp morning air filled with the earthy scent of fallen leaves and the faintest hint of salt from the nearby ocean. The streets of the town were still waking up, with the distant sounds of traffic and the soft murmur of pedestrians mixing with the rhythmic whir of their bicycle wheels on the pavement. Angela felt the exhilaration of freedom as she pedaled alongside Jay, their laughter echoing in the air, a sweet melody punctuating the stillness of the early day. The sun rose over the shimmering Atlantic, the salty breeze whipping through their hair and filling their lungs with the invigorating scent of the ocean. The sound of waves crashing against the shore provided a rhythmic backdrop to their adventure with the warm sun kissing her skin, the thrill of freedom radiating through her.

They followed the winding bike path that snaked through the Hamptons, flanked by charming beach cottages adorned with pastel colors and white picket fences. The air was filled with the sweet fragrance of sun-baked sand and blooming wildflowers, while seagulls circled overhead, their cries mingling with the sounds of the sea. Angela reveled in the beauty of the moment, a sense of peace washing over her as they rode side by side, their wheels crunching over the gravel.

"I know you're worried about me working for your father," Jay began, his voice clear against the backdrop of the surf. "But I promise, I won't let it consume me." He looked at her with sincerity, the glint of sunlight dancing in his eyes.

Angela turned to him, her eyes fluttering with concern. "I just don't want you to feel like you need to impress him. It's okay if you don't want to do this, Jay." She bit her lip, knowing how the weight of expectations could be suffocating, especially in the world her father had created.

"Daniel trusts me now," he said, a hint of pride seeping into his voice. "I'm heading up this deal on my own. It's a big step."

Angela felt an unease in the pit of her stomach at the mention of her father. "I just—" she began, wanting to voice her concerns, but she caught herself, glancing at the sparkling ocean to the side. "Look at that!" she exclaimed, pointing to a group of children laughing as they splashed each other in the surf. "They're having so much fun!"

Laughter erupted between them, but beneath it, an unspoken tension lingered like the distant sound of thunder.

Angela sensed Jay wanted to delve deeper into his new role, but she wasn't ready to confront that reality just yet. The conversation swirled like the sea foam below, momentarily lost in the rhythm of their ride.

Then, in a sudden burst of enthusiasm, Jay mentioned their plans for the following summer. "What do you think about traveling to Italy?" he asked, his eyes brightening. "We could interrail through Italy and end up in Sicily—go back to your roots."

Angela's mind raced at the thought. "That sounds incredible! I've always wanted to see places like Rome, Venice, and Florence." Her imagination took flight, conjuring images of cobblestone streets, vibrant piazzas, and the rich aroma of fresh pasta wafting through the air. "But to go with you would be a dream come true—so romantic."

Jay's smile widened, his excitement infectious. "We could see the Colosseum, toss a coin in the Trevi Fountain, eat gelato overlooking the Amalfi coast, and swim in the deep blue Mediterranean Sea—it would be magical!"

Angela could almost feel the warmth of the Italian sun on her skin, the laughter of locals mingling with the sound of waves. The thought of their adventure together was exhilarating, yet as they cycled on, the dream began to fade into the background, overshadowed by the demands of their daily lives.

As the weeks passed, the busyness of work and college gradually took hold, dimming the vibrant plans for their summer escape. Their grand adventure became a whisper in the wind, barely mentioned, but always lingering in the corners of Angela's heart like a cherished secret, waiting for the right moment to bloom back to life.

Once back in the city, Angela and Jay's life quickly shifted from busy to hectic. Their days were a blur of lectures, assignments, and endless to-do lists. Jay seemed to be juggling even more, with long days at college followed by hours of work, buried in contracts and business deals. If he wasn't poring over paperwork at their apartment, he was downtown in the office, consumed by late-night meetings.

Angela, too, found herself caught up in a whirlwind of planning the Millennium party with Sophie. Every free moment was filled with brainstorming, sketching ideas for decorations, and thinking of ways to make the night unforgettable. The event had become a beacon of excitement for her, something to look forward to amidst the growing distance between her and Jay.

One afternoon, Sophie came over to the apartment, arms filled with rolls of fabric, craft supplies, and a binder bursting with ideas. She tossed her bag onto the couch and sank down next to Angela with a sigh.

"Okay, so for the main room, I'm thinking we lean into a disco theme—lots of sparkle, maybe even a glitter ball," Sophie suggested, flipping through her notes. "But I also love the idea of doing a retro diner look for the smaller room. What do you think?"

Angela nodded, though her mind kept wandering to Jay, who was hunched over his desk in the corner of the living room, his laptop open and a stack of papers spread out before him. She could see the tension in his shoulders, the way he ran a hand through his hair every few minutes.

"Jay, what do you think about the diner theme?" Angela called out, trying to pull him into the conversation. "It'll be fun, right?"

Jay barely looked up. "Hmm? Yeah, sounds good," he muttered, clearly distracted.

Sophie raised an eyebrow at Angela, sensing the disinterest. "We were also thinking of putting up photos from different decades—maybe a wall of memories from the Town's past? Something nostalgic," Sophie added, trying to engage him.

"Yeah, sure. Whatever you want," Jay said flatly, his eyes still glued to his screen.

Angela's patience began to fray. She leaned forward, her voice a little sharper than before. "Jay, you're not even listening. Can you take a minute? This party means a lot to us, and it's kind of important that you're a part of it."

He sighed, a deep exhale that seemed to come from a place of frustration. Without even looking up, he snapped, "I'm working, Angela. I've got a deadline, and I can't concentrate with all this talk about party decorations."

The words hung in the air, cold and unexpected. Angela recoiled slightly, taken aback by the sudden harshness in his tone.

"Jay..." she began softly, trying to suppress the hurt. "I get that you're busy, but this feels like—" She stopped herself, not wanting to escalate things. But the comparison lingered between them, unspoken but heavy.

Jay stood up abruptly, shoving papers into his bag. "I'm heading to the office. I can't focus here," he muttered, brushing past them.

Angela stared at the door as it slammed behind him, the sting of his words lingering in the empty space he left behind. She bit her lip, fighting the rising tide of emotions threatening to overwhelm her. The job, the work, the pressure. It was swallowing Jay whole.

Sophie, always quick to notice, reached over and squeezed Angela's hand. "Hey," she said softly. "Don't let it get to you. He's stressed, that's all. He'll snap out of it."

Angela shook her head, her eyes shimmering with unshed tears. "I just... I don't want him to turn into my dad, Sophie. I've seen how this can go. I've lived it." Her voice wavered, filled with both fear and sadness. "First, it's the late nights, then the deadlines, and then... before you know it, work is all that matters. My dad was never there, and I'm terrified Jay's going down the same path."

Sophie nodded, understanding the gravity of her friend's fears. "I get it, El. I do. But Jay's not your dad. He's got a lot on his plate right now, but that doesn't mean he's going to lose himself in it. He loves you. That much is obvious. He'll come back around."

Angela wiped her eyes and forced a weak smile. "You think so? Because right now, it feels like I'm losing him to the same thing that broke my family apart."

Sophie gave her hand another squeeze. "He's just caught up in the moment. You've seen him when he's with you—how much he adores you. This job is new, and he's probably trying to prove himself, especially to your dad. But trust me, he won't let this become his whole world. Not with you in it."

Angela wanted to believe her, but the doubt lingered, like a storm cloud hovering over the horizon. "I hope you're right," she murmured, leaning back into the couch. "I just don't know how to help him without pushing him away."

Sophie smiled, trying to lift the mood. "Well, you could always throw glitter in his face and remind him about the disco ball," she teased.

Angela chuckled despite herself, the weight on her chest lightening just a little. "Yeah, that might get his attention."

"There you go!" Sophie laughed. "See? It's not all doom and gloom. He'll come around. And in the meantime, we've got a party to plan. Let's make this thing so epic that even Jay can't resist."

Angela took a deep breath, grateful for her friend's optimism. "Okay. Let's do it."

But as Sophie continued flipping through ideas, Angela's thoughts remained on Jay, and the growing distance between them. She just hoped that Sophie was right—that he wouldn't let the work consume him, and that they wouldn't end up on opposite sides of the same wall she had watched her parents build years before.

Isabella's driver pulled up in front of St. Nicholas' convent, the gravel crunching under the tires as the car came to a halt. The building loomed ahead of her, its towering stone facade cracked and weathered with time, casting long, dark shadows across the ground. The convent had always looked imposing, even when she was a young girl, but now, nearly 35 years later, it seemed even more haunting—like a relic from a past she had buried deep within herself. Ivy crept up the sides of the grey stone walls, and the small, arched windows, fogged and dirty, gave the place a ghostly, abandoned feel.

Isabella sat frozen in the car for a moment, her fingers gripping the handle of the door as she stared at the entrance. The wrought iron gates, slightly ajar, groaned in the wind.

She could still remember the first time she had walked through those gates, a 16-year-old girl, naïve and frightened, clutching her swollen belly. She had entered this place full of fear and shame, hoping for salvation, but what she had found inside had broken her. This was the place where her heart had first shattered, where the coldness that would define her for the rest of her life had begun to seep into her bones.

A flashback hit her with startling force. She saw herself, younger and full of quiet desperation, making that long walk up the gravel path to the door, her feet heavy, her body heavier. She had arrived one person and left another—cold, damaged, with nothing but an empty womb and a broken soul. Sister Augusta had warned her all those years ago as she left to heal, to open her heart again before it froze completely. But Isabella hadn't listened. And now, standing in front of this dark, foreboding building, she was back—trying to fix the life that had gone so horribly wrong.

She finally stepped out of the car, the cold wind biting at her skin, and made her way up the path. Every step echoed in the silence. The convent hadn't changed. The same tall, heavy doors greeted her, the same worn stone steps, the same chilling air. As she pushed the door open, the musty scent of the place washed over her, triggering a flood of memories. It smelled of old wood, incense, and something bitter she couldn't quite place—like regret lingering in the air. Inside, it was as cold as ever. The chill wasn't just physical but emotional, sinking deep into her bones as though the walls themselves had soaked up the despair of all the girls who had passed through its halls. The flickering candlelight cast eerie shadows along the stone corridors as she walked toward the office, each footstep echoing back at her.

When she reached the small office, a young nun was sitting behind a desk, her face bright and kind, a stark contrast to the harshness of the convent itself. The nun greeted her warmly, but Isabella could barely muster a smile. The emotions swirling inside her left her raw and vulnerable.

"Good afternoon," the nun said softly. "How can I help you?"

Isabella hesitated, her voice cracking as she spoke. "I... I was here a long time ago. I gave up my son for adoption," she managed to say. "I've been trying to find him, but no one seems to have any records. A private detective told me there's no trace of the adoption. I need answers, please help me."

The young nun listened intently, her eyes softening with sympathy. "I'm afraid we don't have any record of that adoption. Someone—" she paused, her brow furrowing slightly, "—a man came by recently, asking about the same thing. But we couldn't find anything. No files, no records. It's like it never happened."

Isabella's stomach twisted with unease. The weight of the words felt like a crushing blow. How could there be no record? She had been here, she had given birth to her son here. "That's impossible," she said, her voice wavering. "There has to be something. Sister Augusta, she handled everything. She... she must have kept some kind of file."

The nun's expression changed, a flicker of discomfort passing over her face. "Sister Augusta..." she trailed off, clearly hesitant.

Isabella's desperation flared, and she stepped closer to the desk. "Please. I need to know. I've spent too long trying to bury this, but I can't anymore. I need to find him. He's my son."

For a moment, the young nun hesitated, as if caught between her duty and the raw emotion in front of her. She glanced around the empty office before leaning in slightly. "I shouldn't be telling you this," she said in a hushed tone, "but Sister Augusta is no longer here. She's in a care home now, in her 80s. Her memory... well, it's fading. She doesn't remember much."

Isabella's pulse faltered for a moment. A fragile glimmer of hope lit inside her chest, fragile but there. "Where is she?" she whispered, her voice trembling with the weight of years of longing.

The nun quickly scribbled an address on a piece of paper and handed it to her. "I can't promise she'll remember anything. But... you can try."

Isabella took the paper, her hands shaking, and clutched it as if it were a lifeline. "Thank you," she whispered, her voice tight with emotion.

Without another word, she turned and rushed out of the convent, the weight of the past clinging to her like a shadow. As she climbed back into the car, she couldn't help but feel that this was her last chance—her last shot at finding some peace in the wreckage of her life.

"Drive," she commanded, gripping the address in her hand like a lifeline. And as they pulled away from the haunting walls of the convent, Isabella felt, for the first time in years, a flicker of hope.

It was late by the time Jay returned from the office. Angela heard him come in but didn't stir, choosing instead to pretend she was asleep. She lay still, listening to his footsteps move through the apartment, feeling a mixture of frustration and sadness. She couldn't face another argument tonight.

In the morning, Angela woke up early, slipping quietly out of bed before Jay had the chance to wake. She tiptoed around the apartment, grabbed her bag, and left for her classes. The crisp autumn air was a welcome relief as she walked through the city streets, her mind heavy with thoughts of Jay and how things had been lately.

Her classes were the only thing keeping her grounded right now. Mr. Fitzpatrick's lectures, in particular, had become her sanctuary. As soon as she entered the lecture hall, she felt herself relax, the tension from the night before melting away. She loved listening to Mr. Fitzpatrick's stories—he always had incredible anecdotes from his years as a vet, working in remote areas with all sorts of animals. He made the world of veterinary medicine feel alive and full of possibilities.

Angela sat near the front, her notebook open, ready to absorb everything. Today's lecture was on large animal care, one of her favorite topics. Mr. Fitzpatrick was explaining a complex case involving a sick horse when her phone buzzed. A message flashed on her screen. It was from Jay: *"Sorry for the outburst—I didn't see you this morning. Meet you at the café after lectures?"*

Angela sighed softly, feeling a small weight lift from her body. At least he acknowledged he had been unreasonable last night. She typed a quick reply: *"Okay. See you there."*

After her lectures, Angela made her way to the café, her favorite cozy spot near the university. The scent of coffee and freshly baked pastries filled the air as she stepped inside. She ordered her usual—coffee with loads of whipped cream and chocolate sprinkles on top—and found a small table by the window. She pulled out her textbook, trying to focus on her reading, but kept glancing at the door.

Half an hour passed, and still no Jay.

Angela's shoulders slumped. She stirred her coffee absentmindedly, the whipped cream melting into the dark liquid. She was about to pack up and leave when she saw Mr. Fitzpatrick walk in. He spotted her immediately and approached with a warm smile.

"Angela," he greeted, his voice gentle. "You look a bit deflated. May I join you?"

She nodded, feeling a little embarrassed. "Yeah, sure. I was supposed to meet someone, but... they're running late."

Mr. Fitzpatrick sat down across from her, his dark, intense eyes softened by the kindness in his expression. "Well, if you're waiting, I'd be happy to keep you company."

They settled into an easy conversation. Angela admired him—he was an experienced vet with so much knowledge, and yet he always treated her like an equal. She found herself opening up about her dreams, telling him how much she wanted to work with large animals, not just household pets.

"I want to work on the land," she said, her voice filled with quiet determination. "With farm animals, wildlife... I don't know, something more meaningful. I love pets, of course, but there's something about the freedom of working out in the open with animals that really excites me."

Mr. Fitzpatrick nodded, clearly impressed. "That's a fantastic ambition, Angela. It's not easy work, but it's rewarding. And from what I've seen, you've got the dedication and passion to make it happen."

She smiled at his words, feeling a swell of pride. "I just want to learn more. Experience more. I want to be the best I can be."

"You're already on the right path," he replied, his gentle smile reassuring. "In fact, I've been meaning to ask you something. My wife hasn't been feeling herself lately, and she's had to cut down on her hours at the clinic. I could use some help in the evenings. If you're interested, I'd love to have you work with me as a veterinary nurse."

Angela's eyes widened in surprise. "Really? I'd love that! Are you sure I'd be able to help?"

"Absolutely," Mr. Fitzpatrick said, his expression sincere. "You're more than capable. And I think it would be a great opportunity for you to gain some hands-on experience."

Just as they were wrapping up their conversation, the door to the café swung open, and Jay walked in. His eyes immediately landed on Angela and Mr. Fitzpatrick, deep in conversation, and something shifted in his expression—he wasn't pleased.

Angela felt the air grow tense as she introduced them. "Jay, this is Mr. Fitzpatrick, my lecturer. He's been telling me about some opportunities at his clinic."

Mr. Fitzpatrick extended a hand, but Jay's handshake was brief, his smile tight hardly acknowledging him. "Nice to meet you," Jay said, though his tone wasn't friendly. There was an awkward silence before Mr. Fitzpatrick excused himself.

"Well, I'll leave you two to it," he said with a polite nod. "Angela, think about my offer. I'll see you in class."

As he walked out, Jay sat down across from Angela, his body language stiff. She could feel the tension simmering beneath the surface.

"You're late," Angela said, her voice careful. "I've been here for over an hour."

Jay ran a hand through his hair, looking exhausted. "I know, I'm sorry. Work ran late, and I just couldn't focus here with everything going on. I didn't mean to snap last night either. It's just... everything feels like too much sometimes."

Angela looked at him, her heart softening a little, but the frustration still lingered. "I understand you're busy, but I can't help but feel like I'm losing you to all of this. I waited,

Jay, and if Mr. Fitzpatrick hadn't come by, I probably would've left."

Jay sighed, rubbing his eyes. "I know. I'm trying, but it's hard. I don't want to let anyone down—Daniel, the company, you. It's just... so much pressure."

Angela reached out, placing a hand on his. "I don't care about the company. I care about *you*. You don't have to impress my dad or take on all this responsibility if it's not what you want."

He looked at her, conflicted. "I don't want to let your father down either. He's been good to me. He's trusted me with real responsibility. I just don't want to mess it up."

"But what about you?" Angela pressed, her voice soft but firm. "What do *you* want?"

For a moment, Jay looked like he might admit something, his expression softening, but then he shook his head, brushing it off. "I'll try harder, I promise. I'm just stressed. We'll make it work."

Angela nodded, but there was a lingering tension in the air, an unspoken worry that neither of them wanted to fully address. Jay leaned in to kiss her, and she kissed him back, but the moment felt hollow—both of them distracted by the weight of everything unsaid.

The weeks blurred into one another as autumn gave way to winter. The crisp fall air turned icy, and Angela found herself caught up in the whirlwind of the season. Between her studies, work, and the approaching Millennium party, time seemed to slip away. Christmas was nearing, and the buzz of the new millennium filled the city streets, but inside Angela and Jay's apartment, things felt empty. They were like passing ships in the night, rarely seeing each other except for the few exhausted moments in the morning.

Angela had thrown herself even more into her studies, finding solace in the structure of her lectures and the rewarding nature of her new job. After Jay's outburst, she had accepted the position with Mr. Fitzpatrick without hesitation, thinking it would give her something productive to focus on. The apartment had started to feel lonely anyway, and being out of it was a relief.

She absolutely loved working for Mr. Fitzpatrick. He had welcomed her into his practice with open arms, showing her the ropes and treating her like part of the team. Each evening, his wife Shanika would greet her with a warm smile and a hot chocolate when she arrived. Shanika was as kind as her husband, and Angela admired their easy partnership.

"Thank you, Shanika," Angela said one evening, gratefully accepting the steaming cup as she stepped inside the cozy practice. The scent of antiseptic mixed with the rich aroma of chocolate, a comforting combination she was quickly growing fond of.

"You're always welcome," Shanika replied with a smile, handing her a pair of gloves. "Mr. Fitzpatrick is in the back. You two have a few patients tonight, but it shouldn't be too hectic."

Angela followed Shanika down the familiar hallway, feeling the warmth of the building fight off the winter chill. Mr. Fitzpatrick was waiting in one of the exam rooms, finishing up some paperwork. When he saw Angela, he smiled, his dark eyes lighting up.

"Ah, there you are, Angela. Ready for another night?"

"Always," Angela replied with a grin, slipping into the routine.

After they finished the evening's cases, the three of them would often sit together, chatting about life, sharing stories. Angela found herself becoming close to both of them, finding a sense of family she hadn't realized she was missing in the city.

One night, as they wrapped up for the evening, Mr. Fitzpatrick started telling her about his life before New York.

"I actually grew up in Toronto," he said, leaning back in his chair, his voice full of nostalgia. "Shanika and I met at college there. She was studying veterinary medicine too, but she always had a soft spot for New York. We lived in Toronto for a few years after we got married, but when Shanika wanted to be closer to her family, well, I couldn't say no."

Shanika smiled warmly, chiming in. "New York has always felt like home to me. I grew up here, and when we moved back, it felt like everything just clicked."

"Sounds like it was meant to be," Angela said, trying to push the thought of Jay from her mind.

"We've been lucky," Mr. Fitzpatrick replied. "And I have to say, Angela, you've been a great addition to the team. You're doing excellent work here."

Angela smiled, feeling a warmth spread through her. "Thank you. I really enjoy it. I feel like I'm learning so much, and it's exactly where I need to be."

Angela listened intently as they told her more, feeling a pang in her chest as Mr. Fitzpatrick and Shanika shared their story. The ease between them, the effortless understanding that comes with years of love and partnership, was something she longed for. It reminded her of what she wanted with Jay. They had been through so much together—Jay had saved her all those years ago when her world had been unraveling, when she had felt lost and broken. He was the one who had given her hope, love, and a sense of belonging she never thought she would find again. That bond had been strong, and even now, after four years together, she still loved him deeply.

She knew Jay loved her too. It was there in the way he looked at her, even in the small moments when they weren't speaking. They had this connection that ran deeper than anything she had ever known, a connection built on shared pain, healing, and growth. They had fought for their love, built it from the ground up, and she believed in it. She had to believe in it.

Mr. Fitzpatrick looked at her with a fatherly pride, his voice gentle as he could sense she hadn't been herself recently. "You've got a real gift, Angela. I can see you going far in this field."

She blushed slightly, but the compliment filled a space in her heart that had long been empty. Working with Mr. Fitzpatrick felt like she was finally experiencing what it was like to have a father who cared. He encouraged her, listened to her, and genuinely wanted her to succeed. It was everything she had never gotten from her own father.

As the weeks passed, Angela balanced her evenings at the clinic with planning the Millennium party with Sophie. The apartment, on the nights when she wasn't at work, was filled with the chaos of decorations, sketches, and theme ideas spread across the coffee table. Sophie was a whirlwind of creativity, and together they had nearly everything finalized—the invitations had gone out to the whole town, posters were plastered everywhere, and all the decorations and food had been planned and ordered by Sophie.

One evening, as they sifted through some old 80s records they were going to use for the party's theme, Sophie turned to Angela with a grin. "So, what's Jay wearing? Please tell me you convinced him to go full neon."

Angela laughed, rolling her eyes. "I found the perfect outfit for him—bright 80s gear, of course. But he hasn't been around much to try it on. He's been working late again."

Sophie's smile faded slightly. "He's still doing that? You two barely see each other anymore."

Angela shrugged, trying to keep her tone light. "Yeah, but it's just a busy time for him. We're planning to spend Christmas together, so maybe that'll help."

She thought about their upcoming plans—Christmas with her father, Susie, and their little brother Joshua. Angela loved spending time with Jay's family, especially now that little Joshua was old enough to really enjoy Christmas. She couldn't wait for the holidays, hoping it would give Jay a chance to unwind.

"I just hope by Christmas, Jay can switch off and actually enjoy himself," Angela added, her voice betraying a hint of worry.

Sophie gave her a sympathetic smile. "He will. And the Millennium party is going to be amazing. He'll come around."

Angela nodded, though she wasn't entirely convinced.

Later that evening, Angela showed Sophie out as she headed home into the night that was cold and quiet. When she walked back into the apartment, it was dark—Jay wasn't back yet. She stood by the window, looking out at the bustling street below, her breath fogging the glass as she leaned against it.

Memories of her old life, the penthouse apartment, and the cold, distant relationship with her parents crept back into her mind. A shiver went down her spine, but she shook it off.

It'll be fine, she told herself. *It has to be.*

Angela slipped into bed, the sheets cold, and stared at the ceiling, hoping things would change soon.

10

Isabella didn't waste a second. A chill ran through her veins as she pulled up outside the care home where Sister Augusta was now living. The building loomed ahead, a large, faded structure with weathered stone walls. The windows, small and square, were clouded over as if they hadn't been cleaned in years. The air around the home felt heavy, a stark contrast to the city's bustling energy, almost as if the place held the weight of forgotten stories and lives lost in time.

She walked through the entrance, the smell musty with the aging furniture filling her nose as she passed down the narrow hallway. The walls were lined with framed photographs of landscapes—meant to comfort, but instead adding to the melancholy atmosphere. Isabella's chest tightened. She hadn't seen Sister Augusta for nearly 34 years- it felt as though the past was pressing down on her, relentless and unforgiving.

At the back of the room, she saw her. Sister Augusta. She sat in an oversized armchair, so large it looked like it might swallow the frail old nun whole. Her hands, once strong and steady, were now thin and bony, resting on the arms of the chair as she stared blankly out of the window. The world outside was covered in a thin layer of frost, but inside, it felt even colder. The moment Isabella laid eyes on her, memories came rushing back—painful, bittersweet, memories of a time when she had walked the halls of the convent as a scared, pregnant sixteen-year-old girl.

A nurse approached, gently guiding Isabella toward Sister Augusta. As they got closer, the old nun's eyes widened, her face twitching with recognition. Her lips trembled as her eyes filled with tears. "Is that you, dear child?" she whispered, her voice cracked with age but laced with the same warmth Isabella had remembered all those years ago. Isabella couldn't hold back. She crumbled to her knees and fell into the old nun's lap, sobbing uncontrollably. "Sister... I failed."

Sister Augusta stroked Isabella's hair softly, her touch tender and gentle. "You didn't heal that heart, did you?" she said, her voice barely a whisper, but the words cut deep.

Isabella raised her tear-streaked face and begged, her voice shaking. "Please, Sister. I need your help. I need to find him—my son. I need to make it right."

The nurse looked on, her brow furrowed in confusion. "She doesn't usually remember anyone," the nurse murmured softly. But something in Sister Augusta's demeanor had changed; it was as if she had been waiting for this moment, waiting for Isabella to return.

Sister Augusta's face softened, her watery eyes filled with something Isabella couldn't quite place—compassion? Determination? "There is no file," the old nun whispered. "But I'll never forget that house." Her voice grew distant, as if she was drawing from the deepest part of her memory. "I remember the tree... the path..." Her voice trailed off as she described the landscape like a faded photograph coming back into focus.

Isabella listened intently, her body trembling slightly. "Where? Where was this place?"

"A couple of hours from here... a little town. I'll know it if I see it," Sister Augusta replied, her voice frail but certain.

Desperation gripped Isabella. She pulled the nurse aside, pleading. "Please, I need to take her with me. I need to find this place."

The nurse hesitated. "It's not our policy to let residents leave without family permission," she began, but her eyes widened as she recognized who she was speaking to. "You're Isabella Hastings, aren't you?" She spoke as if the name carried weight. Isabella's reputation as a New York socialite, especially after the high-profile hostage incident a few years back, had made her a figure of both fascination and sympathy.

Sister Augusta, her back straightening with newfound purpose, interrupted, her voice firm. "I don't have any family. I've given my life to the church. I have never asked for anything. Let me do this. It's something I need to do."

The nurse glanced between the two women, conflicted but eventually nodded. "Alright. But I'll come with you."

They carefully transferred Sister Augusta into Isabella's car. The journey was quiet, filled with anticipation and nervous energy. The nun was frail, but her spirit seemed alive again, talking in fragments about the path, the trees, the house.

Once they reached the town, they drove for hours, passing large estates and stately homes, but none of them seemed right. Isabella's frustration mounted as the day wore on. She felt the hope slipping away with each wrong turn. "Do you remember anything else?" she asked desperately, her voice thick with emotion.

Then, Sister Augusta's eyes widened. "A stately home... grand... like an old manor." They stopped to ask a passerby for directions, and finally, they were pointed down a winding road about ten minutes outside of town.

As they drove down the pristine, tree-lined street, Sister Augusta's frail hand shot up. "There—the tree!" she exclaimed, her voice trembling with excitement.

Isabella pulled the car to a stop, her heart racing as she stepped out. She stood in front of the grand home, its imposing wooden door towering before her. Could this really be it? Could she be moments away from finding her son? She knocked gently, the sound echoing in the cold air. After a moment, the door creaked open, and a young girl, no older than eight, appeared. "Hello," the girl said shyly. "Are your parents in?" Isabella asked, her voice barely steady.

The girl turned and called for her mother. A tall woman came to the door, wiping her hands on a dish towel. Isabella explained her search, her voice shaking. "I'm looking for a family that lived here 35 years ago... they had a son."

The woman shook her head, apologetic. "We've lived here for 15 years. Before us, it was a family with teenage girls. I'm sorry, I don't know anything about a boy."

Isabella's heart sank. The weight of disappointment felt crushing, but the woman suggested asking the neighbors. They knocked on every door on the street, but no one knew anything. The street had changed, filled with new families who kept to themselves.

Back in the car, Isabella's eyes filled with tears. "I'm sorry, child," Sister Augusta said gently, pulling her into a hug. "Maybe it's time to move on. Your father didn't imagine this for you... you need to let the past go."

Isabella sat in silence, a lump formed in her throat. But then, like a light flickering in the dark, she had a revelation. Her thoughts drifted back to her childhood, to the village in Sicily she had abandoned so long ago. She thought of her mother, her brothers, the farm she had left without a word. The guilt pierced her very being. "I know what I must do," she whispered, turning to Sister Augusta. "If I can't find my son... then I need to make things right with my past. I need to go back to Sicily and ask for their forgiveness. Maybe then... I can finally let go."

11

Christmas seemed to arrive in a flash, bringing with it a flurry of warmth and joy. The holiday season had always held mixed feelings for Angela in the past—her childhood Christmases were a blur of extravagant parties, impersonal gifts, and a house full of strangers. But now, things were different. Angela had finished all her shopping, every present thoughtfully wrapped and ready for a week down at the coast. The excitement for the holidays bubbled inside her, knowing that this year would be filled with love, laughter, and warmth, just as Christmas should be.

Daniel and Susie's house felt a little like home now for Angela. Gone were the sterile, over-the-top decorations she was used to in the penthouse, replaced by warm, inviting lights and festive touches that made everything feel cozy and intimate. A large, real Christmas tree stood in the living room, its branches heavy with ornaments, some of which were handmade by little Joshua with help from Susie. The smell of pine filled the house, mixing with the scent of freshly baked gingerbread and cinnamon from the kitchen, where Susie and her father had been making holiday treats all day. Angela smiled, remembering how different it used to be—cold and impersonal, with staff taking care of every detail, while her parents were too busy hosting socialites and business partners to notice her. But not anymore. Her father had changed, and with her little brother around, the holidays felt like they were finally full of meaning.

Jay had promised to take Christmas off, telling Angela he'd be fully present for the first time in what felt like forever. It made her mind swell with gratitude to think of spending time together again, without the distraction of his studies or his growing involvement in her family's business. They had plans to make the most of the festive season—ice skating at the local rink, visiting friends at the Hamptons, and curling up by the fire as they got closer to a in the new millennium together. Angela couldn't wait to have him all to herself, for the first time in what seemed like months.

But before heading to the coast, Angela had one last celebration. She sat at Mr. Fitzpatrick and Shanika's beautifully set dining table for an early Christmas dinner. The house was like something out of a winter fairytale—candles flickered on the mantle, casting a warm glow across the room, while festive garlands of holly and evergreen draped from the ceiling. Shanika had outdone herself, preparing a traditional Christmas meal with all the trimmings—perfectly roasted turkey, stuffing, cranberry sauce, and even homemade mince pies. The table was adorned with sparkling crystal glasses and silverware, the centerpiece a bouquet of white and red poinsettias. Angela felt like she had stepped into a Christmas card.

They laughed and talked for hours, reminiscing about their favorite patients and joking about how some pets looked just like their owners. Angela felt at ease here, more than she had in any other place in a long time. The Fitzpatricks had become more than just her bosses—they were like family. With them, she didn't feel the loneliness that sometimes crept up on her in the quiet of her apartment.

As they finished dinner and the conversation drifted toward Angela, Mr Fitzpatrick leaned in with a warm smile. "So, Angela, we've told you all about us, but we'd love to hear more about you. How does someone like Angela Hastings, New York elite, end up being such a humble, caring woman?"

Angela felt her stomach tighten, shifting awkwardly in her seat. "My family is complicated, Mr Fitzpatrick," she said softly, looking down at her hands. Mr. Fitzpatrick quickly interjected, "Please, outside of campus, it's Michael and sorry, I didn't mean to put you on the spot."

Angela sighed, feeling a mix of emotions. "It's okay. I'm just... not what people expect when they hear my name. My family—well, they have a lot of history. Secrets." She hesitated, but something about the warmth in the room made her continue. "My mother had a mafia boyfriend she never told us about, and my father... well, he had another family. It was all a mess. I met Jay not knowing who he really was, and then we found out we shared a brother. It was... strange, to say the least. But Jay... he's been my rock through it all. He saved me, more than once."

Her voice softened as she continued, her eyes growing distant. "I've never really fit into the glamorous world they live in. I just wanted a normal life, one where I could help animals and live quietly. That's who I am. All the glitz and glamour... it's never been me."

Shanika reached over and gave her hand a gentle squeeze. "You're doing so well, Angela. You should be proud of yourself."

The evening continued with dessert—Shanika's famous mince pies—and laughter that filled the cozy room. By the end of the night, they exchanged Christmas gifts. Angela's eyes widened when she opened her present from them—her very own personalized veterinary kit, complete with her initials engraved on the instruments. It was thoughtful and perfect, and she was so touched by the gesture that she felt a lump form in her throat.

"I don't know what to say... thank you so much," she whispered, blinking back tears.

Michael smiled warmly. "You're going to be a great vet, Angela. We just wanted you to have something to remind you of where you're headed."

Angela beamed as she handed them her gift—a bespoke sign for their clinic, crafted by a local artisan. The old one had been worn and dated, and she had wanted to give them something that reflected the warmth and care they provided. When they unwrapped it, they were thrilled, hugging her tightly in thanks.

As Angela left that night, she felt lighter, her heart full. Christmas was just around the corner, and for the first time in a long time, everything felt right. With Jay, her family, and her new sense of purpose, she knew the holiday season would be one to remember. And as the new millennium approached, she couldn't help but feel that new beginnings were on the horizon.

12

Angela woke up on Christmas morning to the sound of Joshua's excited giggles as he jumped onto her bed, his eyes wide with wonder. "Get up! Get up!" he cried, bouncing on the mattress. "Santa's been! I can't open my presents until you're up!" Behind him stood Jay, laughing, his eyes twinkling with mischief. It was clear he had orchestrated this little wake-up call, and Angela couldn't help but smile.

"Here," Jay said, handing her a steaming cup of coffee, topped with whipped cream and chocolate sprinkles—just the way she liked it. He leaned down, kissing her softly on the forehead, and whispered, "Better get dressed before Joshua comes back with the water pistol I got him for Christmas." His playful grin was infectious, and Angela laughed, the warmth of the moment settling into her very core. As Jay left the room with Joshua trailing behind him, still bouncing with excitement, Angela took a moment to savor the morning.

She glanced out the window, where the world outside looked like something out of a Hallmark movie. A light dusting of snow covered the lawn, sparkling under the soft morning light. The sky was clear, the air still, and the scene was so peaceful it almost didn't seem real. Inside the house, the scent of oranges and cloves filled the air, mingling with the smell of cinnamon and pine from the Christmas tree downstairs. It felt like the perfect Christmas morning.

Joshua's excitement had brought a new kind of magic to the day. The night before, he had carefully placed milk, cookies, and a carrot by the fireplace for Santa and his reindeer, eyes shining with hope. Angela couldn't help but feel a surge of love for her little brother—he was a blessing in her life, one she hadn't expected but was so grateful for. As she thought about him, a thought crept into her mind: this could be her life one day with Jay. Watching Jay with Joshua, so attentive and loving, she knew he would make an incredible father. She could already picture the future—their own children, holidays filled with the same joy and warmth.

She hurried downstairs, where the living room was already buzzing with Christmas cheer. The tree stood tall in the corner, its twinkling lights reflecting off the ornaments. Joshua was already by the tree, tearing open a brightly wrapped present with pure delight on his face. Angela watched as he let out a squeal of joy, running over to hug Jay. "Thank you, thank you!" he cried, wrapping his little arms around his big brother's neck. Jay smiled warmly, hugging him back.

The presents were handed out, laughter filling the room with each one opened. When it came time for Angela to open her gift from Jay, she was handed an envelope with a large red bow. Her curiosity piqued as she carefully opened it, revealing plane tickets inside. She looked up at Jay, her eyes wide.

"We're going on an Italian adventure this summer," Jay said, grinning. "Just like we always dreamed. Milan, Florence, Rome, and then down to the Amalfi Coast. We'll eat gelato, explore the cities, and relax in the sun. What do you think, Ella?"

Angela's eyes filled with tears. He had remembered. He still cared. The thoughtfulness behind the gift touched her deeply. It wasn't just about the trip—it was about all the memories they had built together, all the dreams they had shared. It was a sign that despite everything, Jay still wanted to be with her, still wanted to create a future together. She smiled through her tears, filled with a renewed sense of excitement for the year ahead.

The rest of the day unfolded like a scene from a dream. They played silly board games, and friends stopped by for drinks and to join in the laughter. The house was alive with the sounds of joy--Joshua running around with his new toys, everyone chatting, music playing softly in the background. Angela felt like she might burst from the love that surrounded her. The food was delicious, a true Christmas feast, and by the end of the day, she thought she would never be able to eat another bite.

But the best part of the day was spending it with Jay. He stayed by her side all afternoon, his hand always resting gently on hers, his presence steady and reassuring. As the sun began to set, casting a soft golden glow over the snow-covered landscape, they slipped outside for a quiet walk together. The cold air nipped at their noses, but Angela hardly noticed, her heart too full of warmth.

They walked along the snow-covered path, the world hushed and still around them, like the quiet of a snow globe. Jay pulled her close, wrapping his arm around her as they made their way down to the water's edge. It reminded her of all those summers they had spent together—just this time, instead of the sun shining down on the beach, it was the soft glow of the setting sun reflecting off the snow.

Jay stopped, turning to her, his eyes full of affection. "I'm glad we're here together, Ella," he said softly, pulling her in for a kiss. Angela shivered as their lips met, the kiss full of the same passion they had shared in those early days, when everything was new and exciting.

As they stood there, watching the last light of the day fade across the water, Angela knew that despite the challenges they had faced, they were still as strong as ever. This Christmas was perfect in every way, and with Jay by her side, she felt ready to take on whatever the new year would bring.

13

Isabella walked into her cold penthouse apartment, the sound of her heels echoing against the marble floors. The expansive windows framed the city below, bustling with life as people hurried about their day. But despite the grandeur of her home, it felt empty and hollow, as if the very walls exuded the chill she felt inside. She sank into the plush sofa, her gaze fixed on the tiny figures moving on the streets below, each one with a purpose, a destination. It only deepened the emptiness in her heart, reminding her of how adrift she had become.

The memories of her childhood back on the farm in Sicily had grown stronger with each passing day. They weren't gentle reminders; they were relentless flashbacks that played over and over in her mind. She could see the sun-drenched fields stretching out endlessly, the scent of freshly harvested olives and lemons filling the air. The adventures she had with her brothers and her best and only friend, Roberto. She could almost hear her mother's voice, calling her name across the fields with that familiar tone—a mix of love and reproach. And in her mind's eye, her mother's face loomed large, the disappointment in her eyes searing straight through her, as if even now, she was saying, *how could you leave us? How could you forget?*

Isabella's chest tightened, her breath catching as the weight of her past settled heavily on her shoulders. Could she be brave enough to return after all these years? To go back to the life she had so desperately wanted to escape? She was scared—more scared than she had ever been. It wasn't the fear of confrontation that haunted her; it was the fear of being utterly rejected, of finding that the family she had left behind had learned to live without her, or worse, had chosen to forget her altogether. She imagined arriving at the old farmhouse, only to find the door closed to her, the windows shuttered against the sight of the daughter who had turned her back on everything she once held dear.

She hugged herself tightly, feeling the raw ache in her heart that had been growing for years. It wasn't as if she hadn't achieved her dreams—she had. She was one of the most beautiful and wealthiest women in New York, her name synonymous with elegance and high society. She had worn the finest clothes, attended the most exclusive events, and lived a life that others could only envy. But none of it had filled the void within her. The constant pursuit of status, the endless search for happiness in designer labels and glamorous parties, had all been for nothing. It was a hollow victory, one that left her feeling even more empty than before.

She thought of the choices she had made—how she had become involved with a dangerous man, given up her child, and then married a man who had never truly loved her. She had convinced herself that she loved Daniel, but now, looking back, she realized they had built a life together on a foundation of lies and secrets. Their marriage had been more of a business arrangement than a partnership, a façade for the world to admire. And in the end, all the lies had unraveled, leaving only a tangled mess of broken trust and shattered dreams.

Her daughters, who had once idolized her, now kept their distance. She could feel their anger and embarrassment in every strained conversation, every sidelong glance. Angela had barely spoken to her since the truth came out about Daniel's affair and the child he had fathered. Francesca, Bianca, and Camilla were polite but distant, their lives moving forward without her. Isabella felt like a ghost in her own family, as though she were being punished for every mistake she had ever made—for leaving Sicily, for abandoning her baby, for pretending to be someone she was not.

Weeks passed in a haze of tears, a kind of sadness that Isabella had never allowed herself to feel before. She was always the strong one, the one who kept her composure no matter what, but now the dam had broken, and she found herself crying for the life she had lost, for the mother she had left behind, and for the woman she had become. She spent hours soul searching; it was as if every regret, every sorrow she had buried deep inside, was finally coming to the surface, demanding to be acknowledged.

She knew what she had to do. It was time to go back to Sicily, but she couldn't just rush in as the broken woman she had become. If she was going to face her past, she had to be stronger, both physically and emotionally. She would spend the next few months preparing herself—getting her body fit and healthy, nourishing herself with good food, and finding some kind of peace in the fresh air outside the city. She started going to the gym regularly, taking long walks in Central Park, and slowly building herself up again. There was a kind of healing in the process, as though she was slowly reclaiming parts of herself that had been lost over the years. When the time was right, she would board a plane to Italy. She planned it out in her mind, envisioning every detail as if to will it into existence. She would spend a couple of months traveling the country, refamiliarizing herself with the language, the culture, the land that had shaped her. She would wander the streets of Florence, lose herself in the art and history of Rome, and soak in the sun on the coast of Naples. It would be a kind of pilgrimage, a journey to reconnect with the girl she had once been before she ever set foot in New York.

And then, when she felt ready—truly ready—she would make her way down to Sicily, to the farm where it had all begun. She would find the courage to face her mother, her brothers, Vincenzo and the life she had left behind. She wasn't sure what she would say, or how they would react, but she knew she had to try. She owed it to herself, to the girl she had once been, and to the family she had left behind.

Maybe then, she thought, she could finally let go of the past and find some kind of peace.

Isabella looked out over the city, the lights twinkling in the distance like a million tiny stars. She took a deep breath, the cold air filling her lungs, and for the first time in a long while, she felt a spark of hope. It was time to go back—time to find herself again, to make things right. It wouldn't be easy, but she was ready to face the journey ahead.

The glorious warmth of Christmas Day quickly faded into a week filled with quiet disappointment. As the days went on, Angela could feel Jay and her father pulling away, retreating into the world of business, where numbers and contracts took precedence over promises and holiday cheer. It was as though the joyous spirit that had filled the house on Christmas morning had been snuffed out, replaced by hushed phone calls and hurried conversations about a big deal set to close in early January. The preparations for the deal consumed more and more of their time, leaving Angela to navigate the week largely on her own.

Jay kept assuring her, in the brief moments they did share, that things would be better once the deal was finalized, and they could finally relax. "Just a few more days," he would say, with a weary but hopeful smile. Yet, each time he said it, Angela felt a familiar sense of dread. She had heard these empty promises before—from her father, who had spent her entire childhood saying that things would be different after the next deal, the next trip, the next year. It had always been *just a little longer* until they could spend real time together, but that time never came. Angela couldn't help but wonder if Jay was becoming just like him, and if she would be waiting forever for a day that never arrived.

Determined not to dwell on the disappointment, Angela threw herself into preparations for the upcoming Millennium party. The whole town seemed to buzz with anticipation, as if they could feel history itself on the horizon. She spent her days helping Sophie in the kitchen, the two of them chopping, stirring, and laughing as they worked to perfect dishes for the celebration. The sweet, buttery scent of freshly baked treats and the sharp tang of citrus punch filled the air, a constant reminder that something festive was coming. They hung garlands of evergreen and gold around the café, strung up twinkling lights, and folded countless paper hats for guests to wear. The decorations sparkled in the warm glow of the café's lights, casting a cheerful ambiance that made it easy, just for a while, to forget about everything else.

In the evenings, Angela would meet up with the old gang, sitting around a fire or squeezing into the cozy café to reminisce about summers past. It was supposed to feel like old times, but there was a quietness hanging over the group, an unspoken tension that everyone felt but no one addressed. Jay's absence was the elephant in the room, a shadow cast over their memories. Angela's friends tried to cheer her up, but she could see it in their eyes—the concern, the pity. They missed Jay too, and they all knew things had changed. Even Sophie, who normally kept things light and cheerful, had moments where her smile faltered, where she glanced at Angela as if searching for the right words to say.

One evening, as they sat around the firepit at the beach, with the cold air nipping at their cheeks, Sophie cleared her throat, breaking the silence. "Remember that time Jay tried to teach us how to surf?" she said with a small laugh. "He was so sure he could get us all up on our boards in one day."

"Yeah, and you ended up with a twisted ankle," Derek added, grinning. "And Jay swore it was because the waves were 'too perfect,' whatever that's supposed to mean."

Angela forced a smile, remembering the way Jay had hovered over Sophie, worried and apologetic, insisting on carrying her back to the shore. "He never did give up on the idea of us all surfing together," she said, her voice soft. "He kept saying, 'Next time, for sure.'"

"Next time," Sophie echoed, her voice tinged with wistfulness. She glanced at Angela, then quickly looked away, poking at the fire with a stick.

As the days went by, Angela spent extra time playing with Joshua, whose innocent joy was a balm to her troubled mind. His laughter filled the house, and his small hands tugged her along as he showed her his newest toys or asked her to help him build a snow fort outside. She found solace in those simple moments—rolling snowballs with Joshua, his cheeks rosy from the cold, or helping Susie bake cookies in the kitchen while Joshua watched, wide-eyed and eager for a taste. Susie never complained about her husband's long hours or Jay's absence; she just seemed content, grateful for her life, her home, and the security she had always dreamed of. Angela admired that about her; Susie didn't need grand gestures or constant reassurances. She was happy with what she had, which made Angela wonder why she herself couldn't feel the same.

Then, a couple of days before New Year's, things came to a head. They were all gathered around the dinner table, the fire crackling in the hearth as the scent of roast beef filled the room. Daniel and Jay were deep in discussion about the upcoming deal, their voices low and serious. Angela was chatting with Susie, half-listening to the conversation at the other end of the table, when a particular phrase caught her attention.

"So, at Bianca's party, you need to be on Mr. Albert. Make sure you're schmoozing him and that he has everything he needs," her father was saying. "This is crucial for the deal—if we don't impress him, we could lose millions."

A chill ran through Angela's veins, her hand tightening around her fork. Bianca's party? That wasn't part of the plan. "Hang on," she interjected, her voice sharper than she intended. "We agreed we weren't going to Bianca's party, Jay. We organized the café party—remember?"

The table fell silent, and Jay shifted uncomfortably in his chair, the color draining from his face. "I know, Ella. I'm sorry," he began, his voice low and hesitant. "But it's important. I'll come to the café later—before midnight, I promise. Let me go to Bianca's first, and then I'll come around 11:30 to ring in the New Year with you. Everyone will be drunk by then, so they won't notice I'm gone."

Angela stared at him, her chest tightening as a familiar anger bubbled up inside her. She swallowed hard, trying to push down the bitterness. "You better be there for midnight," she said quietly. "You need to tell your friends yourself—I don't want to have to do that. They miss you, Jay. Sophie's going to be upset."

"I know, Ella. I'll make it up to them, I swear," Jay said, standing up and leaning over to kiss the top of her head. "I wouldn't miss it for the world."

"You know, Angela," Daniel began, glancing at his plate uncomfortably, "this is the first time Bianca has reached out to me in nearly two years. It's a big step for her to send an olive branch, and I couldn't pass up the opportunity."

"So you had to take it," she said, her voice flat, the words heavy with disappointment. "And of course, Jay has to be dragged along to smooth things over." Her father's face hardened slightly, but she didn't let him speak. "You better not let him miss midnight. He needs to show up for his friends—for me."

Daniel's expression softened just a touch. "I know this isn't what you wanted, but sometimes in life, you have to make compromises. Jay's just helping me with the business—it's important for his future."

Angela shook her head, turning away. "It's always about me compromising though for your business, isn't it?" she murmured. She took a deep breath, her voice trembling slightly as she spoke. "You know, when I was eight years old, there was a show at school where we could showcase a project or piece of art in front of all the parents. I was so excited. I spent weeks making this giant model zoo. I remember begging you to help me with it. I wanted to use the glue gun and nails to make it sturdier, but you kept fobbing me off with promises of 'tomorrow' or 'later.' But tomorrow never came. I waited, and waited, and eventually, I had to finish it myself. I used a glue stick because I didn't know how to use anything else safely, but I knew it wasn't strong enough. Still, I did my best."

Angela paused, her hands gripping the edge of the table as her voice grew heavier. "When the day of the show came, I sat in the wings, waiting and hoping. I kept scanning the audience, searching for you or Mother. Every time the doors opened, I thought, *Maybe this time.* But you never showed up. Neither of you did."

The room grew still, everyone listening intently. Angela's father stared at his plate, his jaw tightening.

"When it was my turn to go on stage," Angela continued, her voice breaking slightly, "I held my head high. I tried to be brave. I stood there in front of all those parents and their kids and explained my model. I wanted you to be proud of me, even though you weren't there to see it. And then—" her voice faltered, her throat tightening as tears welled in her eyes, "it all just fell apart. Literally. The pieces of my zoo crumbled in my hands. That glue stick wasn't strong enough. It couldn't hold it together."

Angela wiped at her cheeks, a bitter laugh escaping her lips. "Everyone laughed. Hysterically. And I just stood there, frozen, completely humiliated. My teacher had to come pull me off the stage because I couldn't move. I couldn't speak. And do you know what hurt the most?" She looked up, her eyes locking on her father. "No one was there to dry my tears. No one was there at all."

Her father flinched, his hands tightening into fists on the table.

"When the show ended, I waited by the school gates, thinking, *Maybe they're late. Maybe they forgot the time.* But no one came. My teacher had to call the house. Then your office. Over and over again. No one answered. So she had to drive me home herself. When we got there, the apartment was empty. No note. No apology. Just silence."

Angela's voice cracked, the pain of the memory washing over her. "I sat on the living room floor and cried until I had nothing left. And that wasn't just a one-time thing, was it? It happened every time I had something special at school. Every recital. Every play. Every achievement that mattered to me. The only times you and Mother ever showed up were for charity galas or events where you needed to look good." The silence in the room was deafening, tension hanging thick in the air. Angela's father finally looked up, his face pale, his eyes clouded with shame.

"I'm sorry," he said hoarsely, his voice barely above a whisper. "Angela, I'm so sorry. For all of it. I can't undo the past, but I am trying. I swear to you, I'm trying to be better."

Angela nodded, her lips pressing into a thin line. "I know, Father. I see it. I see you're trying, and I appreciate that. But do you understand how deeply that kind of pain stays with someone? How much it shapes them? You've apologized, and I want to believe it. But an apology only matters if it's backed by changed behavior."

Her father swallowed hard, his gaze falling to the table again.

Angela took a shaky breath and continued, her voice steadier now. "I can see you're trying to change. But what I

85

can't accept—what I *won't* accept—is you transferring that behavior onto Jay. I love him, but I won't let myself go through this again. I can't. That's why you need to be at this party, Jay."

Her father looked at her for a long moment, his eyes filled with regret and something else—understanding. Finally, he nodded. "You're right," he said, his voice heavy. "I need to do better. Not just for you, but for myself and Jay too."

Angela's heart ached, but she nodded, a tear slipping down her cheek. She wanted to believe him. She truly did. But for now, all she could do was hold onto the power she'd found in herself and keep moving forward.

Jay shifted uncomfortably, his gaze darting toward Daniel with a hint of unease. Finally, he looked back at Angela and said softly, yet firmly, "I'll be there, Ella. I promise."

As Jay got up and took his plate to the kitchen, Daniel spoke up, his voice authoritative. "Meet me in the study in ten minutes, Jared." There was something about the way he used Jay's full name that sent a shiver down Angela's spine. It was as if Jay was already slipping away, being molded into the kind of man her father wanted him to be.

Angela pushed back her chair abruptly, the harsh scrape of wood against the floor cutting through the room. She couldn't sit there a moment longer. It was as if her words had evaporated into thin air—the conversation had shifted seamlessly back to business, as though she hadn't spoken at all. She ran up the stairs to her room, slamming the door behind her. The familiar view of the coast stretched out beyond her window, the fading light casting a silver glow across the water. She sat on her bed, staring out at the wintery landscape, and prayed—prayed for things to go back to the way they used to be, to the easy days of summer when she and Jay were inseparable. She didn't know how much more she could take if things kept going like this, if she kept losing him to the world of business and broken promises. As the first stars appeared in the twilight sky, she whispered to herself, "Please let him come back to me."

15

The day of the party was finally here. After months of preparation and hard work, the café looked breathtaking, transformed into a dazzling time capsule with corners dedicated to iconic decades—the roaring '20s, the rock 'n' roll '50s, the swinging '60s, and the neon glow of the '80s. Streamers hung from the ceiling, vintage posters adorned the walls, and twinkling lights added a festive sparkle to every corner. The food that Sophie had prepared looked like it belonged in a fancy restaurant rather than a New Year's Eve party—bite-sized delicacies and colorful platters that caught everyone's eye. Angela moved around with her camera, capturing photos of the displays and laughing with Sophie about how great these shots would be for her culinary portfolio.

Meanwhile, Derek and Liam were huddled over the sound system, tweaking the settings to make sure the music would flow perfectly throughout the night. "I wonder who's going to get the most drunk and embarrass themselves this year," Liam chuckled as he tested the microphone.

"My money's on old Mr. Parker from the bookstore," Derek replied with a grin. "He's already claimed he's coming dressed as a flapper from the '20s."

Maddie, adjusting the lighting to make sure each decade-themed area was just right, chimed in. "And I can't wait to see what people are wearing for the best-dressed competition. Someone said they're coming as Madonna in full '80s glory. It's going to be hilarious."

Angela joined in, grinning as she checked the last few decorations. "I wonder if the Millennium Bug is actually going to crash all the computers tonight," she joked. "Honestly, I hope it does. That way, Jay won't have any excuse to be stuck on his stupid computer anymore."

Everyone laughed, but there was a hint of tension in the air when they thought about Jay. Angela tried to shake off her unease, promising herself that tonight would be perfect. She slipped out of the café and headed home to get ready for the evening ahead.

As she walked down the hallway at home, she caught sight of Jay through the crack of the door. He was getting ready, buttoning up his tuxedo jacket. Angela paused, peeking in at him for a moment. He looked so handsome and polished, like a grown-up version of himself. But there was something about the tuxedo that didn't feel quite right. This wasn't the Jay she remembered—the boy who would've thrown on a silly outfit and joined her in making a statement. She glanced down at her own clothes, a neon explosion of '80s style, with a fluorescent pink tulle skirt, leg warmers, and sweatbands.

Jay turned and saw her standing there, a smile spreading across his face. "Wow, Ella. You look... very bright," he teased, moving closer to give her a kiss on the cheek. "The café's going to be amazing tonight. You've done such a great job."

"Thanks," Angela replied, a flicker of uncertainty in her voice. "Everyone's worked really hard. I just hope you're actually going to be there, like you promised."

He wrapped his arms around her and pulled her into a hug. "Of course I'll be there," he said softly. "I'm not missing out on a kiss under the disco ball when the clock strikes midnight."

Angela pulled back, looking him in the eye. "I hope so, Jay. I really do."

He gave her one last kiss before stepping away. "I'd better head over to Bianca's now. I'll be back in plenty of time, I promise."

Angela watched as he walked out the door, a lump forming in her throat. She wanted to believe him, but she couldn't shake the nagging worry that tonight might not go as planned.

Angela finished getting ready, taking one last look in the mirror. Her neon pink skirt swished around her legs, and the bright colors felt like a defiant statement—a refusal to let anything dull her night. She made her way out into the crisp night air. As she walked toward the café, she took a deep breath and steeled herself. She had to put on a brave face, to make the most of the night with her friends and the town that meant so much to her. Jay would make it in time. He had to.

When she arrived, the café was alive with energy. The decorations sparkled under the dim, festive lighting. Each corner told a different story from past decades, with vintage records and old posters adding a touch of nostalgia. The smell of delicious food drifted through the air, and laughter spilled out into the streets as people mingled, already giddy with the spirit of the night. The music thumped from the speakers, and the floorboards vibrated with the beat. Everyone was dressed in an array of colorful outfits, from flapper dresses to disco sequins. There was a sense of anticipation in the air—excitement for the new millennium that seemed to buzz through every conversation.

Just as she was about to join her friends, Angela's phone vibrated in her pocket. She glanced at the screen and saw a message from Mr. Fitzpatrick: *"Happy New Year, Angela. Thought we would message early before everything crashes. We look forward to good times for the year ahead."* A smile tugged at her lips, and a warmth spread through her chest. At least someone was thinking about her. Someone cared.

The evening flowed beautifully. The café was packed, and people were embracing the moment. Sophie's food was a hit, with guests constantly complimenting the dishes, marveling at the little details. Derek's guitar set at 10 p.m. had brought the crowd to life, his music weaving through the conversations and pulling people onto the dance floor. Angela couldn't help but feel a sense of pride as she watched her friends shine, their hard work paying off.

But as the night crept closer to midnight, Angela found herself glancing at her watch more often. It was 11:15 p.m.—

Jay should be on his way by now. He'd promised he'd come before the clock struck twelve, and she kept reassuring herself that he wouldn't let her down.

By 11:30, she could feel the nervous energy fluttering in her chest. Every time the door swung open, her heart would leap, only to sink when it wasn't him. She kept a smile plastered on her face, but inside, the hope was fading, giving way to a gnawing dread. The minutes ticked by, and with each one, her doubts grew louder.

At 11:55, her eyes were fixed on the entrance, willing Jay to appear. The countdown began, voices echoing through the café, "Ten, nine, eight..." Each second felt like an eternity, her heart pounding in her ears. "Seven, six..." She glanced around at the faces of her friends, who were stealing worried glances at her. "Five, four..." Still no sign of him. "Three, two..."

As the clock struck midnight, Angela's world seemed to slow down. The café erupted in cheers, balloons and confetti rained down from the ceiling, and everyone around her burst into song, hugging and kissing, ringing in the new year. But Angela just stood there, frozen, the sting of disappointment settling over her like a cold fog. She felt a tear slip down her cheek, unnoticed in the chaos around her.

Minutes passed before she felt arms wrap around her—Sophie, Derek, Maddie, and Liam gathered around, pulling her into a tight group hug. The music blared, and people were laughing and celebrating, but all she could hear was the faint hum of the disappointment ringing in her ears.

Sophie gently wiped away Angela's tears and whispered, "You've got us, Ella. We're here." Then she took Angela's hand and pulled her toward the dance floor, where the rest of the group joined in, surrounding her with love and laughter. They danced under the shimmering lights, their movements weaving together as if trying to mend the pieces of the night.

But as Angela danced, she couldn't shake the feeling that something had shifted. What she had feared all along was playing out in front of her, and the emptiness in the space where Jay should have been felt like a bruise that wouldn't heal.

16

Isabella left for Italy a day after New Year, but this time, it was different. There was no entourage, no driver, no family to accompany her—just herself and one small case, stepping into the unknown. She had shed the armor of Isabella Hastings and reclaimed her birth name, Isabella Verona, a name that had felt like a relic of the past. At first, it was strange to navigate the world without the comforts she had become so used to, but as she stepped outside the Milan airport and felt the cool Italian air brush against her skin, a deep sense of freedom washed over her. This was her chance, her opportunity to atone for all that had been lost and all the wrongs she had committed. She was determined to confront the ghosts of her past and reclaim a piece of herself.

For the first month, Isabella traveled across Italy like a wanderer in search of a home. She traced the cobblestone streets of Rome, listened to the hauntingly beautiful echoes of Florence's churches, and let the gondolas of Venice lull her into a bittersweet nostalgia. But it was on the island of Capri where she finally found a place to rest. The small hotel she chose was modest but charming, tucked away on a hillside with views of the endless blue sea. It became her refuge.

Each morning, she would rise early and stroll down the winding paths to a tiny café hidden among the lemon trees. The air was filled with the scent of espresso and freshly baked cornetti, and the murmur of Italian voices wrapped around her like a forgotten lullaby. Isabella would order her coffee and sit at one of the small iron tables outside, watching life unfold before her. The world felt slower here; time seemed to stretch like the horizon, and every day brought a new discovery. She saw tourists arrive in throngs, pouring off cruise ships with their cameras and eager faces, as if they could drink in all of Italy's beauty with just a glance.

Isabella realized that she had taken it all for granted—the colors, the scents, the rhythm of Italian life. She had lived so long away from it that her own children didn't even speak the language, let alone understand the traditions. Regret pierced her like a knife. What had she done? In trying to craft the perfect life in New York, she had stripped away a part of herself, a part she should have passed down to Angela, Francesca, Bianca, and Camilla. The weight of that loss sat heavy on her chest, but she knew she couldn't linger in sadness if she was to truly heal.

As spring approached, the island burst into life. The cliffs of Capri, crowned with whitewashed villas, gleamed under the sun, and the sea shimmered like liquid sapphire. Bougainvillea spilled over stone walls in vibrant fuchsia cascades, and the narrow streets wove through groves of olive and citrus. Isabella would walk along those paths every afternoon, her footsteps echoing in the stillness. She swam in the ocean, letting the cold water cleanse away years of pent-up sorrow, and watched the fishermen with their wooden boats bobbing in the marina, casting nets into waters as deep and mysterious as her own past.

One crisp morning, Isabella sat at the café as she always did, savoring the bitter warmth of her espresso and the quiet buzz of island life. As she sipped, her eyes wandered over the square, taking in the lively hum of locals and tourists mingling. She was so lost in thought that she barely noticed the elderly man who approached her table, a curious yet kind expression on his weathered face.

"Buongiorno, signora," he greeted, his voice roughened by age but softened by a gentle warmth. "I've seen you here many mornings now, sitting all alone with your coffee. A beautiful woman like you, always by herself... What brings you here, if you don't mind me asking?"

Isabella hesitated, her fingers curling around the small porcelain cup. She wasn't used to sharing her thoughts with strangers, let alone baring the truths she had kept hidden even from herself. But something about the old man's eyes—steady and calm, with a spark of understanding—made her feel as though he might be the one person who could listen without judgment. He would have been the same age as her beloved father, Angelo, had he still been alive—an observation that instantly put her at ease. It felt as if this man had been sent by her father himself, a comforting presence bridging the past and the present, as though he were here to offer the guidance and reassurance she longed for.

She sighed, and her voice came out softer than she intended. "I suppose you could say I'm here to find something I lost a long time ago. Or maybe, I'm here to make up for a life I'm not very proud of," she admitted. "I thought coming back to Italy would help me make amends... but I haven't found the courage to take that final step."

The old man listened intently, his gaze never wavering. He leaned back in his chair and folded his hands on the table. "You know," he began thoughtfully, "when I was a boy, my grandfather used to tell me a story. There was a small village near a great mountain. For generations, the villagers believed that a fire-breathing dragon lived at the summit. They could see the glow of its 'breath' at night and hear the rumbling of its roars. The dragon, they said, would devour anyone who dared to climb the mountain. But at the top of the mountain lay the freshest fruit in the most fertile soil."

Isabella listened quietly, drawn in by the old man's steady voice, as though he were unraveling some long-forgotten truth.

"One day," he continued, "a young boy from the village, tired of living in fear, decided he would climb the mountain and face the dragon. He expected flames and terror, but when he reached the summit, there was no fearsome beast—it was simply a volcano and only a small, old lizard basking on the rocks. The glow the villagers had thought was the dragon's breath was just the lava bubbling in the crater, and the rumbling was the mountain itself, alive with heat and movement."

He gave Isabella a knowing look, his eyes twinkling with wisdom. "You see, signora, sometimes the fears we build up in our minds are like that dragon—fierce and impossible to face. But when we finally gather the courage to climb the mountain, we may find that what we were so afraid of was never a dragon at all. It was just the natural rumblings of life, and the lizard—small and harmless—was the only creature we had to face."

The story resonated deeply with Isabella, and she felt something change. The journey she had dreaded—the one that loomed so large and insurmountable—might not be the dragon she had convinced herself it was. Her fears of returning to her past, of seeking forgiveness, had rumbled like the volcano for so long that she had mistaken them for something more dangerous than they truly were.

The old man rose from his chair, a kind smile softening his lined face. "Good luck, signora," he said, tipping his hat before he strolled away, leaving her to the warmth of the sun and the quiet of the morning.

Isabella gazed into her espresso cup, the dark liquid swirling like the lingering remnants of old fears. She knew it was time to climb her own mountain, to see for herself what awaited her at the top. Whatever lay ahead, it was not the dragon she had imagined, but simply the next step in her journey. And with that realization, she felt a newfound strength begin to emerge. It was time to face her past and finally, truly, let herself come home.

Isabella could no longer ignore the pull of Sicily. It was time to return to the village she had fled from so many years ago—a small corner of the world that had shaped her, whether she wanted to admit it or not. A knot of fear tightened in her stomach each time she thought of it, but she knew there was no escaping the truth.

A week later, Isabella stood on the deck of a ferry as it approached the port of Messina, the first Sicilian soil she had touched since she was a girl of fifteen. Though decades had passed, the essence of the place had not changed. The air was thick with the scent of salt and diesel, and the call of seagulls soared overhead along with the sounds of Vespas whizzing around the bustling streets. She waved down a taxi and gave the driver directions to her village, her voice trembling slightly as she spoke.

The drive was long, winding through hills of verdant green, past rows of vineyards and almond trees, and villages that clung stubbornly to the mountainsides. With each passing mile, the landscape grew more familiar. The sight of the rugged hills and the smell of wild rosemary carried her back to a time when she was young and full of dreams. But now, there was only fear—a fear that grew sharper and more urgent the closer they got.

Finally, the taxi turned down a dusty road, and there it was: the farm. It looked almost untouched by time, the same terracotta roof and faded stucco walls, the same olive groves that stretched out across the hills, though their leaves were not as lush as they once had been. The animals roamed freely along the slopes, their low calls echoing in the distance. As Isabella got out of the taxi, her pulse began to race, her breath catching in her throat. She took slow, hesitant steps up the path, her shoes stirring up small clouds of dust.

The farmhouse loomed ahead, quiet and still. She reached the door and raised a trembling hand to knock, her stomach performing somersaults. The sound of her knock seemed to reverberate through the silence, and after a moment, the door creaked open.

There stood her mother, smaller and frailer than Isabella remembered, but still with the same fierce eyes that had always seemed to see right through her.

"Ciao, Mamma," Isabella whispered, her voice breaking as she saw a lifetime of unspoken words in her mother's gaze.

17

It was 1:30 a.m., and the last guest had finally left the café. Angela and her friends were exhausted but decided to tackle the cleanup now rather than face it in the morning. The air was thick with the remnants of the night's laughter and clinking glasses, but as they began their tasks, a quietness settled over the room. Liam and Derek exchanged stories, laughing over the night's antics, while Sophie was at the counter with her parents, excitedly recounting how well her dishes had been received, relishing the praise she'd gotten from the guests.

Angela moved through the café with a black trash bag in hand, her movements automatic as she picked up discarded plates and cups. Her friends watched her, sensing the weight she carried. She hadn't said much since the night had begun winding down, and while they tried to act normally, they silently agreed to give her the space she seemed to need.

Just then, the door suddenly creaked open, making everyone pause. Angela's heart leapt to her throat as they all turned to see who it was. Jay stood at the entrance, his shoulders slumped, his eyes tired and pleading. He looked as though he hadn't slept in days.

"Ella, can I talk to you outside, please?" he asked, his voice quiet but insistent.

Angela's eyes narrowed, anger flaring up inside her. "Leave me alone, Jay. I have nothing to say to you. Just go away."

"Please, just let me explain," he pleaded, taking a step closer.

She shook her head, her voice growing sharper. "I don't want to hear any of your excuses, because guess what? I've heard them all before. There's no point."

The air grew tense, heavy with the unsaid. The others exchanged glances before Maddie, sensing the need for privacy, cleared her throat. "I think there's still some mess in the kitchen we need to deal with," she said, motioning for the others to follow her.

They hurried out the back, leaving Jay and Angela alone in the empty café, standing on opposite ends of a chasm that seemed to have grown between them.

Jay's voice trembled as he spoke. "Please, Ella—you don't understand how important tonight was for me. I had to be there. You have no idea what it's like... Growing up, I was nothing. I had nothing. We slept on a sofa bed, and there were days when we didn't know if we'd have enough to eat.

Now, I finally have a chance to be something, to make sure that never happens again."

Angela's eyes filled with tears, her anger spilling over into sorrow. "You were never nothing, Jay. You were everything to me. You were kind, and loving, and full of dreams—dreams of teaching and helping people, of being more than just successful. We had plans, remember? We were going to find our own little piece of heaven, where I'd take care of the animals, and you'd start a school to teach kids who needed it most. But now..." Her voice broke as a tear slipped down her cheek. "Now, you're becoming a clone of my father. The Jay I knew is gone."

He took a step toward her, reaching out as if to close the distance. "That's not fair, Ella," he said, his voice strained. "I'm doing this for us, so we can have a better future. If you loved me, you'd understand that. Can't you support me in this?"

She shook her head, her expression filled with a mixture of sadness and resolve. "No, Jay. I know this future— I've lived it, and it is not better, trust me. You know more than anyone that this life—the fancy contracts, the pompous parties—it was my worst nightmare. It's everything I was so relieved to leave behind, and you're choosing it anyway." Her voice softened, but the pain in it was unmistakable. "That tells me everything I need to know. There is more to life than climbing the ladder and rubbing shoulders with people who measure worth by the size of their bank accounts. I thought you understood that, but clearly, I was wrong." Angela took a deep breath and sighed. "I'm just that little 8-year-old girl again, standing on that stage as my model zoo crumbles in front of everyone—completely alone, with no one who cares enough to show up for me when it really matters. But this time... this is the last time. I've had enough."

Jay's face crumpled as he listened to her, his gaze dropping to the floor. "What are you saying, Ella?" he whispered, his voice barely audible.

"I'm moving back to the penthouse," she said, her voice cracking as fresh tears fell. "You can stay in the apartment. I can't do this anymore, Jay. I still love you, but I don't love what you're becoming. I think it's best if we go our separate ways."

Jay's eyes darkened with hurt and suspicion as he searched her face. "You've met someone else, haven't you?" he accused, his voice rising with bitterness. "I thought it was strange how much time you've been spending with that tutor of yours. Were you just waiting for me to slip up so you could be with him?"

Angela's jaw dropped, disbelief flooding her expression as she shook her head. "Don't be so ridiculous, Jay. It's not like that at all," she shot back, her voice firm despite the emotion trembling beneath it. "I work for him—he's my professor. He's been like a father figure to me... like the father I never really had." Her voice softened as she finished, the sorrow in her eyes deepening. "This has nothing to do with him, and you know it. This is about us, about you and the path you're choosing. Please don't make this harder by trying to find someone else to blame."

The rawness in her words hung in the air, but Jay's hurt expression didn't falter. He stood there, stunned and speechless, as if the wind had been knocked out of him. "Ella, please... you're being unreasonable. We can work this out. I'm doing this for us, don't you see that?"

But Angela had already made up her mind. She ached as she spoke the final words. "No, you're doing this for you. There really isn't anything left to say. Goodbye, Jared," she said softly, and then she turned away, clutching the black sack in her hands as she walked into the kitchen.

Jay stood frozen, the weight of her goodbye sinking in like a cold stone in his chest. It felt as though the ground had shifted beneath him, and he was left alone in the dark, facing the consequences of choices he thought were for the best. The emptiness of the café pressed in on him, and the realization hit hard—without Angela and without the support of his friends, this path was something he'd have to walk alone.

He turned toward the door and stepped out into the cold night, the chill stinging his face as he wandered into the darkness, feeling more lost than ever.

18

After the disaster of New Year's Eve, Angela returned to her father's house, her movements heavy with exhaustion. She barely registered the familiar creak of the floorboards beneath her feet as she headed straight to her room. Once inside, she methodically began packing her bag, the weight of her emotions pressing down on her like an anchor. Her fingers trembled as she scrawled a brief note on a piece of stationery: "Thank you for having me." She placed it neatly on the kitchen counter before stepping out into the icy night.

As she approached the city, it was eerily quiet, the remnants of New Year's celebrations flickering in the distance. A few stragglers wandered the streets, their laughter and cheers muted against the stillness. Angela walked through the silence, her thoughts a chaotic whirlwind. Nothing felt real. It was as though she had shifted into another reality, one where joy was inaccessible and the world had lost its vibrancy. She felt numb and unbearably heavy, each step an effort.

Despite everything, she knew she still loved Jay. Desperately. But the clarity that had eluded her in the heat of their arguments now settled like a cold truth: if they continued down this path, heartbreak was inevitable. Jay clung to the life she had worked so hard to leave behind. She couldn't go back, not after everything she'd fought to build for herself. The realization struck her with a sharp pang of sorrow. She replayed the moments of their relationship in her mind, each memory a bittersweet melody of love and loss.

When Angela finally reached their apartment, she unlocked the door and stepped inside. The air felt cold, unfamiliar. The once-cozy space now seemed alien, as though it belonged to someone else. Her gaze fell on the photographs and mementos scattered throughout the living room—reminders of happier times, of laughter and love. Tears began to roll down her cheeks, first slow and quiet, then suddenly in a torrent. A wave of grief crashed over her, knocking her to her knees in the middle of the room. She sobbed uncontrollably, her body shaking with the force of her anguish.

Hours later, Angela awoke curled up on the floor. Her face was sticky with dried tears, and her limbs ached from the awkward position. For a fleeting moment, she hoped it had all been a cruel nightmare, but the stark reality hit her like a blow. She had a long day ahead—packing up the apartment, arranging her move, and preparing to return to her mother's home. It was the last place she wanted to go, but she had no choice. School was overwhelming, with assignments and exams looming. There wasn't time to find another place to live.

Angela worked methodically, stuffing her belongings into boxes and bags. She avoided looking at the photographs again, the trinkets that told the story of their life together. When Isabella's driver arrived at the door, she felt a pang of finality. She locked the door behind her, leaving behind the memories, the laughter, and the heartbreak. The elevator ride to the penthouse felt interminable, each floor taking her closer to a future she dreaded.

When the doors slid open to reveal the apartment, Angela froze. Isabella stood there, her usual cool demeanor replaced by something unrecognizable. Her expression was soft, open, even tender. Without a word, she held out her arms, inviting Angela into an embrace. Angela hesitated for only a second before stepping forward, allowing herself to be enveloped in her mother's warmth.

To Angela's astonishment, tears sprang to her eyes, and she began to cry, her emotions spilling over uncontrollably. Isabella tightened her hold, her own tears glistening as they fell silently. They stood there in the doorway, mother and daughter, sharing a moment of raw vulnerability. The walls that had always separated them seemed to crumble in an instant. Angela felt something she hadn't realized she had been longing for her entire life from her mother—connection, understanding, love.

As their tears subsided, they remained entwined, each taking comfort in the other. Angela's heart ached, but it was no longer from despair. In that embrace, she felt a glimmer of hope—a promise that perhaps, despite everything, she wasn't entirely alone. Together, they could begin to heal.

After what felt like hours, Isabella gently ushered Angela into the living room. The fire crackled softly, casting a warm glow over the elegant furniture. It was a stark contrast to the whirlwind of emotions swirling inside Angela, but the unexpected tenderness in Isabella's expression gave her pause. They sat side by side on the plush cream sofa, and for once, Angela felt as though she could open up to her mother.

At first, it was strange—almost unsettling. *Who was this imposter, and what had they done with Isabella Hastings?* But as the minutes passed, Angela's walls began to crumble. Slowly, hesitantly, she started to talk.

She told Isabella everything.

About Jay—how he'd changed, how he let her down time and time again, and how much it hurt because she still loved him. She recounted the disaster of the New Year's Eve party, her voice trembling with suppressed emotion. Anger spilled out, but so did sadness, and before she knew it, she was reliving the years of love and heartbreak with her mother sitting quietly beside her.

Isabella listened—really listened—and it was as if Angela were seeing her for the first time. Gone was the polished socialite who rarely had time for anyone but herself. In her place was a woman who seemed open and unguarded, who responded with reassuring knee squeezes and empathetic nods.

When Angela's words finally ran dry, Isabella reached for her hand and held it tightly. She gazed at her daughter with tear-filled eyes and said, her voice trembling yet steady, "My darling, it breaks my heart to see what your father and I have done to you over the years. For that, I am truly sorry."

Angela froze, shocked by the uncharacteristic vulnerability in her mother's tone.

"The way we raised you," Isabella continued, "made you feel like you were never good enough. We created this belief in you that someone else's love, approval, or affection made you worthy. And that was our greatest failure." She exhaled deeply. "I see how much you love Jay. He's been a wonderful part of your life, someone who made you feel seen and loved. But now... things have changed. You've been giving your power to him, letting him dictate your happiness."

Angela blinked, her throat tightening.

"You did the right thing ending it," Isabella said softly. "Who knows what the future holds? What I have come to realise is that endings are also beginnings—it just depends on the way we look at it. I was very fond of Jay, but what matters now is you. You need to start believing in yourself. You don't need anyone to save you, Angela. You don't need anyone else's approval or love to prove your worth."

Isabella paused, her gaze distant for a moment, before returning to Angela's. "This is something I'm learning for myself. When we think this is where love ends, it is actually where love begins, but this time for ourselves. All my life, I was searching for adoration, for admiration—always from others. But by looking outside of myself, I never found it. I made terrible mistakes. Marco treated me like a trophy, and I gave away my baby because I was desperate for fame and to be adored. Your father never truly loved me, no matter how hard I tried to make him, and I failed as a mother because I was always chasing something outside of myself."

Angela swallowed hard, her mother's words hitting her like waves.

"What I've realized," Isabella continued, "is that everything we need is already within us. It's up to us to fill our own cups, to love ourselves, and to follow what lights our souls on fire. Depending on others to do that only gives them the power to make or break us. And when we take care of ourselves, when we follow our passions, the right people will come into our lives as a bonus—not as the foundation for our happiness."

Angela stared at her mother, stunned.

"The tighter we hold onto things, the more likely we are to lose them," Isabella said gently. "So, we have to let go and focus on what we can control—ourselves. Caterpillars embrace transformation, knowing that every ending is just the beginning of something new—a chance to become a beautiful butterfly. Now it's your turn. Cocoon yourself in growth, trust the process, and when the moment is right, spread your wings and soar."

Angela suddenly felt overwhelmed, her emotions swirling like a storm. Her mother's words struck deep, peeling back layers of insecurities and self-doubt she hadn't even realized she carried. For so long, she had yearned for a moment like this—for a motherly chat, for wisdom, for warmth. Now that it was happening, it was almost too much to process.

Her mother's message was profound, and painfully true. Angela had spent her life searching for worth in others' eyes—whether it was her father's approval, Jay's love, or even her sisters' admiration. But the truth was, her worth had always been within her.

Her mind wandered to her studies and her job with Mr. Fitzpatrick. The veterinary work had brought her immense joy, and it had led her to friendships that felt easy and real. Mr. Fitzpatrick and his wife had welcomed her with open arms, their kindness as natural as the bond they shared. Angela hadn't needed to fight for their affection or prove herself to them—it had simply happened. That thought filled her with a quiet sense of pride.

After a long silence, Isabella's gaze shifted to the beautifully packed suitcase in the corner of the room. She sighed and turned back to Angela with a small, bittersweet smile.

"That's why I'm leaving."

Angela's eyes widened in disbelief at her mother's words. *Why now?* Angela thought. Just as she was beginning to feel the warmth and love she'd always craved, her mother was going away. But then, Isabella's earlier wisdom came rushing back: *We have to do this ourselves.* Her mother had her own path to walk, just as Angela now had hers.

Angela took a deep breath, her voice trembling as she asked, "What do you mean you're leaving? Where are you going?"

Isabella sighed softly and picked up her suitcase. Angela stared at it, momentarily distracted by how small it was. It seemed so unlike her mother, who usually traveled with trunks upon trunks of designer clothes, as though she were packing up an entire life.

"I'm going to Italy," Isabella said quietly. "And then to Sicily. I have a lot to put right, Angela. I've made so many mistakes in my life, and now it's time to make amends. It's time to find out who I truly am and what I truly want from life."

Angela listened intently, her soul aching at the vulnerability in her mother's voice.

"I tried to find my lost son," Isabella admitted, her voice breaking slightly. "But it was impossible. He's gone, and I have to accept that. It's out of my control. But there's still time to make things right with my family in Sicily. I don't regret leaving them—I know that life wasn't for me either—but the way I left... it was wrong. Just slipping away in the middle of the night, without a goodbye, without ever reaching out again. That wasn't fair to them."

Isabella's gaze dropped to the floor, her usually confident demeanor softened with regret.

"I'm going to spend the next few months traveling through Italy," she continued. "I want to reconnect with the culture and the life I left behind. Then I'll go to Sicily to see my family. If you ever feel like joining me, you're more than welcome. I've left the address on the counter." Isabella glanced at her daughter, her eyes shimmering with unshed tears. "I'll keep in touch. But for now, it's time for me to go."

Angela rose to her feet and stepped forward, wrapping her arms around her mother in a tight embrace. "Thank you," she whispered into Isabella's ear, her voice thick with emotion.

They stood there for a moment, holding each other, before Isabella gently pulled away and smiled. Angela watched as her mother picked up her suitcase and disappeared down the hallway.

As the apartment grew quiet again, Angela felt a spark ignite within her. She knew what she had to do now. This was her time—not Ella and Jay's time, just hers. She would focus on her studies, on her work, and on her dreams of working with animals out on the land, far away from the chaos of the city.

For the first time in months, Angela felt truly fired up about the future. She was ready to find herself, to take back her power, and to forge a path that belonged solely to her. This was her moment. And she wasn't looking back.

20

Isabella stood frozen as her mother stared through her, the woman's expression as blank and cold as the spring wind biting at her face. It was as if Isabella didn't exist, as though she were a ghost from a past her mother refused to acknowledge. Isabella tried again, her voice trembling. "Ciao, Mamma... may I come in?"

Her mother's response was as brutal as it was final—a sharp, echoing slam of the door. Isabella flinched, the sound hitting her stomach like a physical blow. She stood there motionless, the weight of her past mistakes and her mother's rejection pressing down on her. Seconds ticked by, though they felt like an eternity, before the door creaked open again.

Franco, her eldest brother, stood in the doorway. His face was a mixture of disbelief and cautious anger. "Is that really you, Isabella?" he asked, his voice rough, like he'd swallowed years of hurt and bitterness.

Isabella's composure broke. Her shoulders shook as she bowed her head and let out a soft, broken cry. Through her tears, she looked at him, searching for any trace of the strong, vibrant brother she once adored. But Franco had changed. His once robust frame was now frail, and the light in his eyes had dulled, replaced by the weight of a life that had not been kind.

"What are you doing here?" he asked, his voice low but firm. "Why now, after all these years? Mamma buried you in her heart long ago. To her, you don't exist anymore. Do you even understand the damage you left behind? We didn't know if you were alive or dead, Isabella. If it weren't for Zia Rosa telling us you made it to America, we would've thought you'd disappeared forever. You have no idea what that did to us—what it did to her."

Isabella wiped her face with trembling hands, her voice raw with desperation. "I know, Franco. I know I've done terrible things, and I'm here to make it right. I need to apologize—to Mamma, to you, to everyone. Please, let me in. Let me explain. Let me try to fix this."

Franco hesitated, the door still partially closed, as if he were shielding their home from the storm she had become. He sighed, a long, heavy sound of resignation. "Mamma won't hear it. You know how she is. She's too stubborn, too hurt. She won't even let you step through this door."

A sinking feeling came over Isabella, but Franco continued, softening slightly. "Look, Roberto in the village has a spare room. I'll take you there for now. You can stay a few days while I try to talk to Mamma. Tonight, Mario and I will come to see you, and you can tell us everything. But don't think this will be easy. You didn't just leave us, Isabella. You shattered this family. And it's not just us. You left a mess behind you in this village. A lot of people were hurt—people like Vincenzo and his family."

The mention of Vincenzo sent a fresh wave of guilt washing over Isabella. The man she was supposed to marry, the man whose life she had upended with her sudden departure. Her voice wavered. "Vincenzo..."

Franco gave her a pointed look. "Yes, Vincenzo. He's moved on, Isabella. He married a good woman, and they have a family now. But you broke something in him when you left. It wasn't just you running away—it was you running from a promise. People don't forget things like that. And now you'll be staying with Roberto, do you remember, Vincenzo's younger brother?"

Isabella blinked in surprise. "Roberto?"

Franco nodded. "Yes, Roberto. He owes me a favor, and he has a spare room and it's away from the farm. You can stay with him for now, but don't think for a second this absolves you of what you've done. If you're serious about making amends, you'll need to face them too. All of them."

Isabella nodded slowly, the weight of her brother's words sinking in. She knew he was right. Her betrayal hadn't just hurt her family; it had rippled through the lives of others, leaving scars she had tried to ignore.

Isabella nodded, tears streaming down her face. "Thank you, Franco. I don't deserve your kindness, but thank you.

I'll explain everything—I promise. I'll do whatever it takes to make it right."

Franco studied her for a moment, then gave a small nod. "Let me grab my coat. I'll take you to Roberto's."

Isabella hesitated, her voice soft. "I don't want to impose, Franco. It might be awkward staying there. I can stay at a hotel."

Franco let out a dry laugh. "A hotel? This isn't New York, Isabella. The closest thing we have to a hotel is Vincenzo's barn, and I doubt you'd enjoy sharing it with his goats."

As Franco went inside, Isabella stepped to the edge of the cliff, the sweeping hills and rugged coastline of her childhood stretching before her. The familiar scents of the sea and wild rosemary tugged at her memories. She gazed down at the spot where she'd seen her father's lifeless body all those years ago, the day her world had crumbled.

She turned to the weathered bench they used to share, where he'd once dreamed aloud with her about her bright future. Those dreams had carried her across oceans and into a world she once thought would fulfill her, but now they felt hollow. Achieving them had come at a cost—a cost she hadn't fully understood until now.

Lost in thought, she didn't hear the soft footsteps behind her until she felt a hand on her shoulder. Turning, she saw her brother Mario. His face, though marked by the passage of time, still held the familiar warmth and charisma she remembered so vividly. His caring eyes met hers, brimming with tears.

Without a word, he pulled her into a tight embrace, his emotions spilling over. "Isabella," he choked out, his voice breaking. "Where have you been? I've missed you so much."

The guilt and sorrow Isabella had kept locked away for years surged forward, crashing over her in waves. Her body shook as she sobbed into her brother's shoulder. "I'm sorry," she whispered, her voice barely audible. "I'm so, so sorry."

Mario held her tighter, his tears mingling with hers. "We've all been waiting for this moment, Isabella," he said softly. "I just hope it's not too late."

And for the first time in decades, Isabella felt a slight thawing of her heart.

21

Angela took a while to adjust to life back in the penthouse. It wasn't the loneliness that unsettled her—she had spent most of her childhood navigating the echoing emptiness of those walls. What ate at her was the realization that now, it truly was just her. No one to lean on, no one to share the weight. Her mother's words echoed in her mind, reverberating for weeks. Isabella had been right—Angela had spent her entire life as a victim of her circumstances, waiting for love and approval to fill the voids left by her parents, her sisters, her peers, and even Jay.

Jay had been the first person to really see her, to make her feel worthy, and she'd poured her entire sense of self into their relationship. But now, she realized how dangerous that was—her happiness had hinged on someone else's presence and validation. That had to stop. This was about her now, about loving herself, knowing her worth, and building a future she could be proud of without depending on anyone else to pave the way.

Angela threw herself into rediscovering her independence. She focused on her studies, her job at the clinic with Michael and Shanika, and reconnecting with her friends. Occasionally, she'd catch herself checking her phone, hoping for a message from Jay. But each time, she forced herself to stop. That was the old Angela—this new Angela understood boundaries and refused to be an afterthought in anyone's life. If Jay couldn't give her what she deserved, it wasn't her job to beg for it. He was entitled to have his own dreams now, they just no longer aligned with what she wanted so there was no point.

The months that followed were transformative. Angela delved deeply into her past hurts and traumas, working hard to heal them. She established a new routine: every morning, she spent time visualizing her future self, immersing herself in the life she aspired to create. She pictured herself in a cozy, sunlit home nestled in a small, picturesque town. Outside, rolling green fields stretched endlessly, dotted with animals she cared for—a mix of rescued strays, farm animals, and wildlife she rehabilitated. In her vision, she was surrounded by love: a caring husband whose gentle laugh filled the room, and children whose happy chatter echoed through the halls. She saw herself hosting family dinners on the porch, the table laden with food, the air filled with warmth and laughter.

Angela imagined her days filled with purpose and peace, tending to her animals in the morning, walking through the dewy grass as the sun rose, and spending the evenings reading stories to her children or enjoying quiet moments with her husband. She could feel the soft breeze on her skin, hear the rustle of leaves in the wind, and smell the comforting aroma of fresh earth after the rain. This life was everything she wanted—not glamorous or grand, but simple, honest, and full of meaning. Each detail of this vision brought her a sense of hope and freedom, a reminder of the life she was working toward—a life built entirely on her own terms.

After her morning routine, Angela would take a brisk walk in the park, shower, and head off to college. Afternoons were spent at the clinic, learning alongside Michael and talking about their shared hopes for the future. By evening, she'd return home to study, closing each day feeling stronger and more in control of her life than ever before.

22

Months passed and on an unusually cold April day, Jay spent the entire night tossing and turning, his mind replaying the last six months in an endless loop. Every mistake, every regret, every choice that had led him to this moment haunted him. His gaze drifted to the plane ticket sitting on his bedside table, its crisp edges catching the faint moonlight filtering through his window. Destination: Italy. It had been a whirlwind few days, but the regret now hit him with the force of a tidal wave. What had he done?

He had thrown away everything that mattered to him.

After Angela had ended things, he had buried himself in work with Daniel. Late nights, endless meetings, early mornings—anything to escape the ache in his chest. But in doing so, he had neglected everything else, including his studies. The foundation of his future had crumbled beneath him as his grades plummeted. He thought he could outrun the pain, but three days before, it had all come crashing down.

The head of his faculty had called him in for a meeting. Her voice had been firm but not unkind as she delivered the news: he had failed his classes. To pass, he would need to repeat the year.

The words had struck him like a thunderclap.

In that moment, sitting in her office, the enormity of his choices finally hit him. His future had unspooled in his mind—a bleak vision of living Daniel's life, the same one Angela had described so vividly: empty, shallow, heartless. And then, for the first time in years, Jay completely broke down.

The tears came without warning, hot and uncontrollable, pouring from a place he hadn't even known existed. His head of faculty had been understanding, her tone softening as she encouraged him to take a break. "There's no point continuing the finals," she said. "You've already failed this year. Use the time to figure out what you want. Come back fresh when you're ready."

Now, as Jay sat up in bed, clutching the plane ticket in his trembling hands, a flicker of hope sparked in his chest. Maybe it wasn't too late. Maybe he could fix things with Angela. They could still go to Italy together, just like they had always dreamed.

He would tell Daniel in the morning that he was quitting. This life—this relentless pursuit of wealth and status—it wasn't for him. Angela had been right all along. He had enough savings from the deal he'd closed after New Year to get by for a while, long enough to figure out his next steps.

He glanced at the clock: 11:30 p.m. It was late, but he couldn't wait another moment. He needed to see Angela, to tell her everything, to beg for her forgiveness. He had been such a fool, chasing after something that had never mattered and losing the one person who did.

Throwing on a hoodie and jeans, he ran out into the cool April night. The city buzzed faintly in the background, but Jay barely noticed as he flagged down a passing taxi. The ride to Angela's apartment felt both agonizingly slow and far too fast.

When they arrived, he jumped out and hurried down the familiar street. His heart pounded in his chest as he rehearsed his speech in his mind, the words tumbling over each other. But as he turned the corner to her building, he froze.

There she was. Angela.

But she wasn't alone.

Under the soft glow of the streetlamp, she stood in the arms of another man. Jay's breath hitched as he recognized him—her professor, Mr Fitzpatrick. The embrace wasn't casual. It was warm, intimate, and it shattered something deep inside him.

His legs felt like they might give way as he stumbled back, retreating into the shadows. He watched for another moment, his heart sinking further with each passing second, before tearing his gaze away. His stomach churned, and the bitter taste of heartbreak rose in his throat.

She had moved on.

Jay turned and walked away, his pace quickening until he was nearly running. The cool night air stung his face, but it couldn't numb the pain tearing through him. By the time he reached his apartment, he was gasping for breath, his chest heaving with a mix of exhaustion and despair.

He collapsed onto his bed, the plane ticket still clutched in his hand. It was over. Truly over. Angela had found someone else, and he had no one to blame but himself.

As sleep finally claimed him, his dreams were a cruel reminder of what he had lost. He saw the life they could have had together—lazy mornings wrapped in each other's arms, adventures across Europe, a future full of laughter and love. But it was only a dream, fading into the darkness as he slipped further into sleep.

When morning came, Jay knew what he had to do. He would pack his bags and head straight to the airport. Italy awaited—a place to clear his mind, to start over, to figure out who he was without Angela.

But as he stared at the ticket one last time, he couldn't shake the feeling that no matter where he went, he would always be running from the ghost of the life he should have had.

23

Easter weekend couldn't have come at a better time for Angela. The break was a welcome relief after the relentless pace she had been keeping with her studies and work.

One late April evening, just before Easter, as she scrambled to complete her essays for the end of her second year, Angela hit a wall. No matter how hard she tried, she couldn't get one of her essays right. The panic bubbled inside her as the hours ticked by. At 9 p.m., with the essay due first thing in the morning, she picked up her phone and called Michael.

"Hi, Michael. I'm so sorry to bother you," Angela said, her voice shaky. "I'm completely stuck on my essay, and I don't know what to do. Could you help me figure it out?"

Michael immediately heard the panic in her voice, and guilt pricked at him. Had he pushed her too hard, both in class and at the clinic? "Of course, Angela," he said gently. "How about I come over right now? We'll work through it together. It's the least I can do after all the extra hours you've put in for me."

"Are you sure? I don't want to impose..."

"I'm already grabbing my coat," he replied. "I'll be there in no time."

True to his word, Michael arrived swiftly. Together, they sifted through textbooks, articles, and notes, piecing together the essay one step at a time. By midnight, it was done, and Angela finally felt a sense of calm and gratitude wash over her. She walked Michael to the door, the cool April air hitting her face as they stepped outside.

Out of nowhere, a wave of emotion surged, and tears began to spill down her cheeks. "I can't thank you enough for tonight, Michael. You really saved me. I think I've just been so caught up in everything that I didn't realize how much I still had left to do. It all just hit me."

Michael wiped away her tears with a reassuring smile and pulled her into a protective hug, kissing the top of her head. "Angela, you don't have to carry everything on your own, even the strongest people have moments of weakness." he said softly. "I know you're working so hard to be independent, and I admire that. But asking for help doesn't make you weak. It's okay to lean on people who care about you. Me, Shanika—we're here for you, no strings attached. That's what real kindness is."

Warmth radiated from him, and Angela felt a deep gratitude settle in her chest. She'd been so focused on building her independence that she hadn't realized how much having people like Michael and Shanika in her life truly enriched it. As she watched Michael disappear into the night, she stood on the steps of the building, her body feeling a little lighter. For the first time in a long while, she felt like she could balance strength and vulnerability—and that was its own kind of power.

Yet, as she folded her clothes into her overnight bag, getting ready for the Hamptons, a wave of dread washed over her. She had been invited to her father's house for an Easter egg hunt and lunch, and she wasn't looking forward to it.

Angela hadn't set foot in the Hamptons since the disaster that had been New Year's Eve. Her father had invited her countless times since then, but she always had an excuse—too much coursework, a shift at the clinic, or simply needing time for herself. The truth was, she hadn't been ready to face the place, the memories, or, most of all, Jay.

But she knew she couldn't avoid it forever. Sooner or later, she would have to face him. After all, he wasn't just her ex-boyfriend—he was also her stepbrother.

She dressed carefully, choosing an outfit that understated but still flattering. She wanted to look nice without making it seem as though she was trying too hard. It was just a day visit, and she was grateful for that. The thought of staying overnight at her father's house felt suffocating, so she had made plans to stay with Bianca at their family's Hamptons house instead. It had been ages since she'd last visited, and the thought of seeing her sister helped ease her nerves.

Angela picked up the carefully wrapped Easter treats she'd bought for Joshua and made her way to the waiting car. Louis stood by the door, his posture slightly more rigid than usual.

"Morning, Miss Angela," he greeted her warmly, though she caught a flicker of sadness in his eyes. He had driven for Isabella for nearly two decades, and with her now being in Italy, he seemed lost without his usual routine. Angela often tried to make him feel needed by asking him to drive her places, even though she was perfectly content using the subway or a taxi.

"Morning, Louis. I hope you're ready for a long drive," Angela said with a smile, hoping to lift his spirits.

"It's been a while since we've taken this road," Louis replied, holding the door open for her. "The Hamptons is quieter this time of year. Shouldn't be too long."

As the car glided down the near-empty roads, Angela's mind was far from quiet. She couldn't stop thinking about Jay. For weeks, she'd managed to push thoughts of him to the back of her mind, consumed by the demands of her veterinary program. But now, the memories came rushing in, bringing with them a familiar ache.

Last Easter, Jay had been the life of the party. He'd loved hiding eggs in the garden for Joshua, delighting in watching the little boy's excitement as he dashed from bush to bush. Later, they had stuffed themselves with chocolate, laughing as Jay pretended to be in a sugar coma. Those moments had been so joyful, so easy.

Angela bit her lip, her stomach twisting. What would it be like to see him now? Would he be cold? Polite? She resolved to keep things civil. They were adults, after all, and they would have to coexist.

When the car pulled into the driveway of her father's house, Angela hesitated before stepping out. Memories flooded back—of the first time she'd arrived here, brimming with hope and dreams for a future with Jay. How naïve she had been.

The big white door opened before Angela could knock. Susie stood there with a bright smile and arms outstretched. "Angela! It's so good to see you," Susie said, pulling her into a warm embrace. The sincerity in her voice instantly helped Angela relax.

"Hi, Susie. It's been too long," Angela said, feeling a pang of guilt. She hadn't visited in months, too caught up in her own world.

"Joshua's been asking for you all morning. He's missed you so much," Susie said as she led Angela inside. "How have you been, darling?"

"I've been good, just so busy with school and work. I've been looking forward to today, though," Angela replied, her voice tinged with guilt.

"Well, come on in. We're all out in the garden," Susie said, ushering her through the house.

Angela stepped into the garden and stopped in her tracks. It was like stepping into a scene from *Alice in Wonderland*. The lawn was dotted with colorful decorations—oversized teacups, whimsical signs, and pastel-colored bunting. Children darted around with Easter baskets, their laughter filling the air, while parents mingled by a table covered in craft supplies for bonnet-making.

"Wow, Susie, this looks amazing," Angela said, genuinely impressed. "Did Jay do all of this?"

Susie's face fell slightly. "Oh, thank you, dear, but Jay didn't do the decorations this year. Your father handled everything. Don't you know? Jay isn't here."

Angela blinked, confused. "He's not here? Where is he?" Susie hesitated. "I thought he would have told you. He left about a week ago. Called Daniel in a terrible state and said he couldn't work for the company anymore. He... he left for Italy, Angela. Said he was using the ticket you two had planned to use together."

The words hit Angela like a punch to the gut. Her lungs felt tight, and she struggled to catch her breath. "Italy?" she echoed, her voice barely above a whisper.

Susie nodded. "I think he needed to get away, clear his head. I think he's doing the itinerary you planned at Christmas."

Angela excused herself and hurried to the bathroom, her mind racing. Jay had left school? Quit the job he'd fought so hard for? Why? Why now? And why hadn't he come to her?

She stared at her reflection in the mirror, willing herself not to cry. Her throat burned with the effort of holding back tears. "Get a grip, Angela," she whispered, fanning her face with her hands.

When she returned to the garden, she focused all her attention on Joshua, who beamed with delight at her presence. She laughed with him, helped him find eggs, and did her best to enjoy the day.

Still, the weight of Jay's absence lingered, and when the party finally wound down, Angela was relieved to retreat to the car.

"How did it go, Miss Angela?" Louis asked gently as they drove away. "Your sister's waiting for you at the house. She said she's got hot chocolate ready."

A wave of dread washed over Angela. All she wanted was to crawl into bed and be alone, but she knew she couldn't brush Bianca off. As they pulled into the driveway of the Hamptons house, she saw her sister waiting on the porch, arms crossed with a playful grin.

"Hooray, my sister finally visits!" Bianca teased.

Angela stepped out of the car, forcing a smile. "Hey, Bianca. I heard you've got hot chocolate waiting for me."

"You know it. Come on, spill everything. You've been avoiding me for too long," Bianca said, linking her arm with Angela's and leading her inside.

Angela took a sip of her hot chocolate, savoring the rich, creamy warmth as she curled up on the couch. Bianca sat across from her, her feet tucked under her, holding her mug with both hands. The soft glow of the fireplace cast a comforting light over the room, but Bianca's intense look suggested her thoughts were anything but serene.

"Father and I have been talking more," Bianca began, her tone hesitant.

Angela looked up, surprised. "Really? That's...unexpected. How's it going?"

Bianca exhaled, her lips pressing into a thin line before she spoke. "It's been...hard. Really hard, Ang. I'm not going to lie. After everything that happened—Mom, Jay, the way he treated us all—it's not easy to just forgive and forget. But he's trying. I think he regrets a lot, and for the first time, I feel like he actually wants a real relationship with me."

Angela nodded slowly. "That's a big step. He's not the most emotionally available person, but if he's making an effort, that says something. How do you feel about it?"

Bianca shrugged. "Conflicted, honestly. Part of me wants to tell him it's too little, too late. But another part of me thinks...maybe this is a chance to start fresh. I've been thinking about joining him at the company."

Angela blinked in surprise. "You? Working with Father?"

Bianca laughed softly. "I know, it sounds insane. But hear me out. If I'm there, I can keep things grounded. Make sure he's actually listening to people, not just steamrolling over everyone like he usually does. Maybe I can help him see things differently. I think he needs a lawyer's input too. And, selfishly, it might be a way for us to rebuild something."

Angela reached over and squeezed her sister's hand. "Bee, that's an amazing idea. You'd be great at it. And honestly, if anyone can keep Father in check, it's you. He needs someone like you—someone who isn't afraid to stand up to him. Plus, you really know your stuff!"

Bianca smiled, her expression softening. "You really think so?"

"Absolutely," Angela said firmly. "You've always been the strong one. If this feels right, you should go for it."

Bianca nodded, her gaze thoughtful. After a moment, she tilted her head and looked at Angela. "Enough about me. What about you, Ang? How are you holding up...with Jay?"

Angela's heart sank at the mention of his name. She took a long sip of her hot chocolate, as if it could steel her nerves. "He's in Italy," she said quietly.

Bianca's eyes widened. "Italy? What? When? Why didn't you tell me?"

Angela shrugged, trying to keep her voice steady. "He left about a week ago. Susie told me at the Easter lunch. Apparently, he's following the itinerary we planned together."

Bianca frowned. "Wait, hold on. He just up and left? What about his job with Father? School?"

Angela shook her head, her throat tightening. "He quit everything. Told Father he couldn't do it anymore. I don't know. I don't understand why he didn't come back for me. Why he went without me. It's like he's just...gone."

Bianca set her mug down and leaned forward, her expression intense. "Ang, listen to me. If you want something, you have to go after it. Sitting here and wondering won't change anything."

Angela looked up, her eyes filling with tears. "But what if he doesn't want me there? What if he's moved on?"

Bianca's voice softened, but her words were firm. "And what if he hasn't? You won't know unless you ask. Don't make the mistake Camilla did. Now look at her- she's lost!"

Angela frowned. "What do you mean?"

Bianca sighed, a wistful look crossing her face. "Bradley. She loved him, Ang. More than anything. But she let him go without a fight. I thought she was being strong, letting him choose his path, but deep down, she was scared. Scared of rejection, of looking foolish. And now? He's with someone else, married, living a life she'll never be part of. She regrets it every single day."

Angela stared at her sister, the weight of her words sinking in.

Bianca reached over and took Angela's hand. "Don't make the same mistake, Ang. If Jay is your Bradley, go to Italy. Find him. Ask him why. Fight for him. You only have a few essays left, right? You can do those anywhere. Go to Italy, and if nothing else, you'll have your answer."

Angela swallowed hard, her pulse quickening. "You really think I should?"

Bianca smiled, squeezing her hand. "I don't just think so—I know so. Go find your Jay, Ang. Don't wait until it's too late."

Angela nodded, a spark of determination lighting up her eyes. Maybe Bianca was right. Maybe it wasn't too late to find her own happy ending.

24

Isabella and her two brothers made their way across the village toward Roberto's house. As her shoes crunched against the cobblestone paths of her childhood, Isabella felt a whirlwind of emotion. Every corner, every building seemed to whisper fragments of her past. Villagers paused mid-conversation to watch her pass, their murmurs barely concealed. It was as if time had stood still in Villa Montana, preserving its sights, sounds, and gossip exactly as they were when she'd left.

The weight of the stares pressed down on her shoulders. Thirty-four years away hadn't erased her presence from their memories, nor had it dulled the sting of her departure. A shiver ran up her spine as they approached the familiar piazza, bustling with morning life. She longed for solitude—

a quiet, anonymous hotel room where she could hide and gather herself. Instead, she was being led straight to Vincenzo's brother, Roberto. Staying with him felt wrong, even intrusive, and she couldn't shake the fear that she wouldn't be welcome.

Her brothers led her down a narrow alleyway that fell silent, a stark contrast to the lively square. The air here was cooler, the buildings taller, creating a cloistered calm. They stopped outside a tall stone townhouse with weathered shutters and a large rooftop terrace adorned with a pergola. Grape vines spilled over its edges, their tendrils swaying gently in the breeze. Mario knocked loudly, his fist echoing against the heavy wooden door.

"Roberto! Open up!" Mario called out.

The sound of clattering footsteps traveled down the staircase inside, and moments later, the door creaked open, and there he was—Roberto.

Isabella's breath caught in her throat. For a moment, she was transported back in time. The playful boy she remembered stood before her, now a man. His green eyes sparkled in the sunlight, framed by lines that deepened as he smiled. His dark hair was tousled, as though he'd just rolled out of bed. Yet that boyish charm hadn't faded.

"So, the prodigal sister returns!" Roberto said, his grin widening. His voice was warm, teasing. "How are you, Isabella? You haven't changed a bit."

Before Isabella could respond, he pulled her into a hug. The scent of coffee and sun-dried cotton clung to him, grounding her in the present.

"I'd recognize you anywhere," he continued, stepping back to look at her. "What brings you back? Tired of all that traffic and those skyscrapers in America?"

Franco cut in before Isabella could react. "Very funny, Roberto. But we don't have time for this. I need to get back to the farm. Can Isabella stay here for a bit? Mamma won't have her there."

Roberto's brows arched, but his grin remained. "Well, we can't exactly leave her on the street, can we? That'd be rude, even for us. Of course, she's welcome. Here, let me take your bag."

He reached for her suitcase before Isabella could protest. "Come in, make yourself at home."

Isabella hesitated, glancing at her brothers as if they were abandoning her. But she stepped inside, and to her surprise, the house wasn't at all what she expected. Instead of the dark, cluttered bachelor pad she'd imagined, it was bright and airy. The walls were white, and the furniture was simple and modern. Olive trees stood in terracotta pots, and colorful paintings of Sicilian landscapes brightened the space.

Roberto disappeared into the kitchen while Isabella sat stiffly on the sofa. She stared out the window, unsure of what to say or how to feel.

"Espresso?" Roberto's voice called from the kitchen.

"Yes, please," Isabella replied. "I could use a strong one."

Moments later, Roberto appeared with two small cups balanced on a tray. "We'll have these, and then I'll show you the rooftop. You're going to love the view. Though, I'm not sure how it'll compare to your New York penthouse."

Isabella froze, her head snapping up to meet his gaze. "How do you know where I live?"

Roberto laughed, his green eyes twinkling. "Everyone knows where you live, Isabella. You might be a world away, but magazines travel, you know. You've been the talk of this village for decades. The name Isabella Verona isn't mentioned lightly around here, but believe me, it's mentioned plenty. Everyone wanted to know what happened to the girl who left Villa Montana behind."

Isabella's cheeks burned with embarrassment. "Gosh, you don't pull any punches, do you?"

Roberto leaned against the arm of the sofa, his expression relaxed. "Why would I? I've got no reason to sugarcoat things. Honestly, I always found it funny how much your leaving shook this place. Your mamma was livid, my brother Vincenzo was furious, and even my dad felt scandalized. All that fuss over a girl chasing her dreams."

Isabella's eyes flickered with surprise. "You didn't think it was a big deal?"

He shrugged. "Not really. I thought it was brave. You did what everyone else here probably dreamed of but was too scared to try. That's what really upset them—they envied you. Doesn't bother me what you've done or where you've gone. So relax, Isabella. I'm not here to judge."

Isabella's rigid posture softened at his words. Roberto handed her the espresso and gave her a playful wink.

"Come on," he said, gesturing toward the stairs. "Let's go upstairs. You've got to see my view."

As she followed him, coffee cup in hand, Isabella felt a spark of intrigue. Perhaps returning home wouldn't be entirely unbearable after all.

25

Angela couldn't stop replaying Bianca's words in her mind as the car wound its way back to the city. The conversation had stirred something within her. Despite their differences and the strain between them since the revelations about their dad, Angela could see her sister was on a path to healing. Bianca was starting to figure out her own future, and the decision to work with their father—perhaps even take over the Hastings Empire—was a huge leap. It wasn't the Bianca she'd known growing up, the one who seemed so preoccupied with appearances and control.

Angela sighed, resting her forehead against the cool glass of the car window. Francesca was another story. Their oldest sister was practically a ghost in the family, living her glamorous life in France with her husband and baby. Every invitation to come home was met with excuses—"the baby's schedule," "Pierre's work commitments." But Angela knew the truth. Francesca was avoiding them, avoiding *him*. Their dad's new wife and the brother close in age to her own child were wounds she wasn't willing to poke at.

And then there was Camilla. Angela frowned. Her other sister had retreated into a life of mystery, keeping her work and personal life so tightly guarded that it felt like she had vanished. Angela didn't even know where she lived these days. The absence of her sisters weighed heavily on her. Growing up, she'd dreamed of a big, united family—one where they could all gather around a table, laughing, sharing stories, and being *real* with one another. But the Hastings family had never been like that. Their dinners were formal, stiff affairs, with tension bubbling just beneath the surface.

That's why she had always imagined a different kind of life with Jay. A home filled with warmth, love, and laughter—a safe haven from the coldness she'd grown up in. But now, as she imagined him traveling through Italy, her chest ached. What if he met someone else? Someone effortlessly beautiful, the kind of girl who fit seamlessly into his new life abroad? Jay was charming, funny, tall and undeniably handsome. Angela had no doubt that girls would be drawn to him like moths to a flame.

Her stomach twisted at the thought. She hated feeling this insecure, this powerless. Her mother's words echoed in her mind—she didn't *need* anyone to make her whole. And that was true. These last few months, she had learned so much about herself and what she wanted from life. She was stronger than she'd ever been. But even so, her dreams always came back to Jay. Could she let him go without even trying to fight for them?

Bianca's voice rang in her ears, a quiet plea wrapped in Camilla's own regret. Losing Bradley after the prince disaster had been one of the greatest mistakes of her life. She had let her pride stop her from chasing after him, and now he was married to her old best friend. "Don't make the same mistake Camilla did," Bianca had said.

Angela stared out the window at the rows of houses rushing past. For a fleeting moment, she saw her future—a house full of light and laughter, her children running through the halls, and Jay standing at her side, his smile as steady as ever. She knew better than anyone how regret could fester. Her mother was proof of that. Past mistakes had haunted Isabella for decades.

Angela took a deep breath. Bianca was right. She had just a few essays left to finish, and then school would be done for the year. Summer stretched out in front of her like a blank canvas. Michael would understand if she needed to step away for a while. He had always been kind and supportive.

For the first time in weeks, she felt a spark of purpose ignite inside her. She wouldn't sit by and let life happen to her. She would spend the next week tying up loose ends—completing her schoolwork, wrapping up her commitments at the clinic—and then she'd pack her bags. By next weekend, she'd be on a plane to Italy.

If Jay had moved on, then at least she would know. She could face the truth and finally start a new chapter in her life, free from the what-ifs. But if there was even the slightest chance they could find their way back to each other, she had to take it. Angela straightened in her seat, her resolve hardening.

No more waiting. No more fear. It was time to fight for what she wanted.

26

Angela sat on the plane, a wave of warmth rushed through her as she waited for take-off. She had spent the day before on the phone, calling everyone she thought needed to know about her sudden decision. Her father and Susie had been far from enthusiastic. Their words echoed in her mind, gnawing at her confidence.

"Don't you think you should give him some space, Angela?" her father had said, his voice calm but firm. "He seemed in a bad way when he called to say he was leaving. I've never heard him like that, and neither has his mother."

Angela had tried to push the conversation aside, but it lingered. If Jay had truly hit rock bottom, then didn't he need her now more than ever? Apart from the final months of their relationship, he had always been there for her when it counted, and she wanted to do the same for him. It stung, though, that he hadn't tried to win her back, not even a phone call or a letter. Maybe he thought her words had been too final, or maybe he was afraid of rejection.

When she landed in Italy, Angela pulled out the schedule they had sketched together after Christmas—a hopeful plan that had once filled her with so much excitement. She had skipped Milan and Venice, flying straight to Rome to catch up with him. By now, he had to be there. She knew finding him would be tough. No-one had heard from him in a long time. Angela had tried his phone countless times but he had probably left it at home as it was unlikely to work abroad.

As soon as she stepped out of the cab in Rome, the city overwhelmed her senses. The air was alive with the aroma of fresh pasta and roasted coffee, mingling with the distant hum of traffic and the chatter of tourists. Though she had traveled to glamorous destinations with her mother and sisters, they had never come to Italy. Yet as Angela wandered the lively streets, she felt an inexplicable connection, as if she had arrived home.

Her hotel was a quaint little building near the Trevi Fountain, and from her small balcony, she could see the throngs of visitors below. Couples kissed, children made wishes, and laughter filled the air. As dusk fell, Angela noticed a young girl, about her age, toss a coin into the fountain. A single tear rolled down her cheek. Angela's heart clenched. What was the girl wishing for? Love, perhaps, or the return of someone lost—just like Angela.

When she woke the next morning, she was hit with a wave of panic. She didn't have a proper plan. Jay could be anywhere in this sprawling city. The itinerary they'd written together was vague, just a list of cities and rough dates. With no hotels booked and no leads, Angela realized finding him was like chasing a shadow. But she refused to give up just yet.

She spent her days exploring Rome, stopping at every breathtaking landmark. She visited the Colosseum, strolled through the Vatican, and climbed the Spanish Steps, gelato in hand. Every night, she showed Jay's picture around, asking if anyone had seen him. But no one had. Still, Angela tried to focus on the journey itself. This wasn't just about Jay—it was a chance to reconnect with her roots, to walk the same streets her mother might have once walked as a young fashion model.

After a few days, she moved on, traveling down the Amalfi Coast. The winding roads revealed stunning views of turquoise waters and colorful cliffside villages. She stopped in Positano, Ravello, and Sorrento, savoring the beauty and indulging in fresh seafood and limoncello. Each town felt like stepping into a postcard, but her search for Jay remained fruitless.

In Naples, Angela felt her hope beginning to wane. Weeks had passed, and she hadn't heard a single whisper of him. She wondered if he had fallen in love with one of these enchanting places and decided to stay—or worse, if he had met someone new. Exhausted from the constant travel and living out of a suitcase, she found herself at a crossroads.

Needing a moment of stillness, she stepped into a centuries-old church, its towering stone walls offering a quiet refuge from the bustling streets outside. The scent of melting wax and aged wood filled the air, and the flickering candlelight cast shifting shadows across the marble floor. As her eyes adjusted to the dim glow, she noticed a figure standing at the front of the church, his back to her.

Tall. Broad shoulders. Blonde hair catching the soft, golden light.

Her breath hitched. *Jay?*

Anticipation coiled in her chest, making her pulse quicken. She took a careful step forward, then another, her heartbeat hammering in her ears. The world around her faded into silence as she approached the altar, her footsteps hushed against the worn stone floor.

Just a few more steps.

She reached out, her fingers trembling as she gently tapped his shoulder.

The man turned.

Angela's heart plummeted. It wasn't him.

A rush of embarrassment burned through her as she forced a polite smile, murmuring an apology before retreating. Disappointment crashed over her like a wave, leaving her hollow and aching. The fragile hope she had clung to for so long now felt foolish—like chasing a dream that had already slipped through her fingers.

Days later, sitting by the port in Calabria, she stared at the boats swaying gently in the water. Failure clung to her, but a new thought began to take shape. Her mother would surely be in Sicily by now, reconnecting with their family. Angela's pulse quickened at the idea. Maybe this was what she was meant to do—join her mother, meet the family she'd never known, and help rebuild the bonds Isabella had shattered so many years ago.

Excitement coursed through her as she rushed to the ticket booth. She pulled out the address of the farm she had tucked into her bag before leaving. Sicily felt like the answer she hadn't known she was looking for. The idea of a summer on the island, surrounded by family and its vibrant culture, filled her with hope.

It was nearly the end of May, and Angela knew she couldn't search forever. But maybe, just maybe, this journey wasn't about finding Jay at all. It was about finding herself—and Sicily was where she needed to be.

27

Isabella had been in Villa Montana for weeks now, and her mother still refused to see her. Each morning, she would rise early and retreat to the roof terrace, captivated by the stunning vistas. Roberto had been right—it truly was like nowhere else in the world. From her perch, she could see for miles, the rolling hills stretching into the horizon. On clear days, the volcanic islands loomed in the distance like ancient sentinels.

She watched the birds soaring effortlessly through the sky, envying their freedom. As a young girl, she had taken this beauty for granted, too wrapped up in the daily grind of working in the fields. Picking fruit, feeding animals—it had been grueling, and Isabella remembered how her fingers would bleed and her back would ache by the end of the day.

She had never doubted her decision to leave, but sitting here now, the weight of regret pressed on her chest. How much of her family had she missed by cutting them out of her life so completely?

Each morning, Roberto would bring her coffee and a pastry, and they would sit together on the terrace. He had been her anchor, grounding her with his easy-going nature. They talked for hours, reminiscing about their childhood and the days when their families' farms bordered each other. Isabella found herself clinging to his stories, filling in the gaps of her fragmented memories. Roberto took Isabella on a journey through their shared past and beyond, revisiting their old haunts and exploring places she had never seen before. They wandered to secluded beaches, swimming beneath the stars in perfect solitude. Together, they toured volcanic islands and savored fresh fruit plucked straight from the trees.

Though Isabella's family refused to see her, she cherished every moment of being back in Sicily, reconnecting with the beauty of her homeland—and with the dear friend who made it all feel like home again.

"So, how is your brother?" Isabella asked one morning as, a wry smile tugging at her lips. "I'm sure he found a wonderful woman. Trust me, I wouldn't have made a good wife for him."

Roberto laughed, leaning back in his chair. "He was angry and embarrassed when you left—heartbroken, though he'd never admit it. He married a few years later. Do you remember Marla? Lovely woman, but they have a fiery relationship. They argue constantly, but somehow they make it work. They've got two children now, Giorgio and

Carla. Well, not children anymore—they're probably around the same age as your girls. But if I am honest, and he'd kill me for saying this, I don't think he ever got over you."

Isabella sighed and a knot formed in her stomach- a knot of guilt. She had missed so much. Tonight, Roberto was taking her to dinner at his family's farm to see his brother Vincenzo and his parents, Carlo and Maria. Though she longed to see them, she dreaded the encounter. Would they welcome her or resent her for dredging up old wounds?

Roberto had been a breath of fresh air. His kindness and humor had made her feel at home in a place that had once been filled with pain. When villagers whispered as she passed, he would loudly crack a joke to ease her discomfort. "What a scandal, Isabella," he'd say with mock seriousness. "I can't believe you've come back to fight your brothers for the farm!" The villagers would gasp, and Roberto would chuckle, muttering under his breath, "That'll give them something to gossip about."

His acceptance was a comfort to her soul, a reminder of the carefree friendship they had shared as children. "Your mother was always kind to me," Isabella said later that afternoon, a soft smile playing on her lips. "When she saw me struggling in the fields, she'd sneak me into your house, hand me a cold glass of lemonade, and let me read her magazines. I think you take after her."

Roberto gave her a sideways glance and grinned. "She's still the same. Always helping others. She wasn't angry when you left, you know. She understood. She told my father to calm down, that it wasn't the end of the world. It took time, but she even softened him. Your brother, though—Franco—he's had a tough time."

"What do you mean?" Isabella asked.

"When you left, your family struggled to keep the farm running. It was too much for your mamma, and in the end, my family bought the land. My parents did their best to be fair—they let your family keep living there, in their house and paid them a decent wage for working the fields. They made it a bigger, more successful farm, but for Franco and Mario, it wasn't easy. They were used to being in charge, and working for Vincenzo—a younger man, no less—was a hard pill to swallow. Franco especially hated taking orders. He felt humiliated, like his pride was stripped away. He'd always thought he knew better, and being subordinate has been a constant source of tension. But my family truly did what they could under the circumstances. It wasn't perfect, but we all had to make it work."

Isabella's heart ached at the thought of her brothers enduring such bitterness and frustration. "It sounds like your family did the best they could," she said quietly.

Roberto nodded. "We tried. It's pride, Isabella. Pride always cuts the deepest. But now..." His voice trailed off, and his expression darkened.

"What is it?" Isabella pressed.

"They have bigger problems now," Roberto said with a sigh. "Have you heard? A corporation wants to buy the farm. The land is prime for development—tourism, hotels, you name it. Vincenzo's been struggling to keep up with loan payments, and if the bank forecloses, they'll lose everything. Generations of work, gone."

Isabella's pulse faltered for a moment. "I could help," she said quickly. "I have the money. It's the least I can do."

Roberto looked at her intently. "I know you mean well, but be careful. Offering money could wound some egos—especially Vincenzo's and Franco's. They're proud men. But if anyone can find a way to help, it's you."

Determination flared in Isabella's chest. She *would* find a way to save the farm. This was her chance to make things right, to rebuild the bridges she had burned.

Roberto broke her thoughts. "Come on, Isabella. Time to face your past." He grinned, helping her to her feet. "Don't worry. I'll protect you."

She gulped down the last of her coffee and gave him a look of mock dread. Roberto laughed, and his warm presence gave her the courage to take the next step.

Isabella held on to Roberto's arm as they walked up the stone path to his family's farmhouse. The uneven cobblestones beneath her feet mirrored the uneven rhythm of her heart. As they neared the entrance, the door swung open, and Vincenzo stood there, blocking their way. His piercing glare shifted from their linked arms to her face, an unspoken accusation flashing in his eyes.

"So, are you going to let us in, or are you just going to stare us down all night?" Roberto broke the tension with a laugh, stepping forward. "Lighten up, Vin! She won't bite."

He shoved his brother lightly, but Vincenzo stood firm, his tall frame rooted like an ancient tree. Finally, with a huff, he stepped aside just as Maria appeared behind him.

"Isabella, bella!" Maria's voice was warm and effervescent, her arms already outstretched as she approached. Isabella blinked, taken aback. Maria was nothing like the frail, elderly woman she had imagined. Instead, she was vibrant and strong, her dark, curly hair streaked with silver, her movements youthful despite her years.

Before Isabella could react, Maria enveloped her in a hug so tight and loving it stole her breath. It was the kind of embrace she hadn't felt in decades, one that reminded her of Zia Rosa's—full of warmth and the unspoken promise of home.

"I am so happy you came back to us," Maria said, pulling back to look at her. "Look at you— so elegant, so chic! We have so much to catch up on." She kissed Isabella on both cheeks before turning sharply. "Vincenzo! Stop standing there like a bodyguard. Come in and welcome our guest!"

Roberto jabbed his brother in the arm, grinning as he dragged him inside. "You heard Mamma—chill out!"

The evening was overwhelming for Isabella. The farmhouse was filled with life, laughter, and curiosity. She met Marla, Vincenzo's wife, and their children, Giorgio and Carla, who were polite and warm despite Vincenzo's lingering hostility. The conversation was relentless, with Vincenzo and Carlo bombarding her with questions about her glamorous life in New York.

Roberto did his best to deflect the tension, cracking jokes to steer the conversation toward lighter topics. But no matter how many laughs he drew, the questions returned, sharp and probing. Isabella found herself dancing around her truths, carefully omitting Marco, the son she had given away, and her strained marriage with Daniel. Instead, she focused on her daughters, her pride in them, and her desire to find a new purpose.

Finally, Isabella couldn't hold back any longer. She took a deep breath and stood, her voice trembling as she addressed the room. "I need to say something. I need to apologize to you all."

"Darling Isabella, there's no need," Maria interjected, but Isabella held up a hand.

"No, I need to clear the air." She hesitated, her gaze dropping to her hands. "I'm sorry I left without a word. My father's death shattered me, and I didn't know how to cope. Staying here was too painful. I thought I'd call once I was settled, but shame kept me away. I was ashamed of the choices I made, the life I lived... And as the years passed, it became harder and harder to reach out. I know it's too little, too late, but I want to make amends. I want to help."

The words hung in the air like a fragile glass bauble, ready to shatter. Vincenzo rose from his seat, anger flashing in his eyes. He opened his mouth to speak, but the sudden chime of the doorbell cut him off.

Maria rushed to answer it, and moments later, Isabella froze as her mother and brothers entered the room. Her mother's expression was stormy, her steps hesitant, as though she had been dragged there against her will.

Her brothers approached her first, kissing the top of her head in greeting. But her mother stayed at a distance, her glare icy.

"I have come to talk to my daughter," Caterina announced, her voice cold. "You are not welcome here, Isabella. The Lombardo family has been good to us. Even after you rejected their son, they let us keep the house and work the farm. You abandoned us, and now you think you can waltz back in as if nothing happened?"

Isabella's stomach churned, but she stood her ground. "I know I made mistakes, Mamma. I'm here to say sorry and to try to make things right."

"Make things right?" Caterina's voice rose. "You had everything you needed—a home, food, family—and it was never enough for you! You were selfish!"

Isabella's voice cracked as she replied, "I wasn't trying to hurt anyone, Mamma. I just wanted something different. I know I handled it wrong, but I couldn't live the life you chose for me. I'm sorry..."

Her mother slammed her hand on the table, her face turning red. "And who are you to talk about choice? Did you think about our choice when you left? Your brothers worked their hands raw to keep the farm going, and the Lombardos—bless them—they let us stay out of pity. But we were the ones who bore the shame, Isabella. You humiliated us."

Isabella froze as a familiar wave of guilt washed over her. "I never meant to humiliate you, Mamma. I just wanted a different life. Is that so hard to understand?"

Her mother's glare hardened. "Hard to understand? What good did all that 'different life' nonsense bring you? You threw away family for what? A failed marriage? Shame on you!"

The words struck like a blow, and Isabella staggered under their weight. Angela's face flashed in her mind, the echoes of their fights reverberating in her ears. This fight had sounded familiar. *Had she become her mother?* She swallowed hard, her voice breaking. "You're right. I've made mistakes. But I'm here now to help, to do whatever I can to make things better. I have means to save the farm."

"What? With your money?" Vincenzo spat, rising to his feet. "Of course Roberto told you! Always running his mouth off. We don't need your pity or your handouts, Isabella."

"It's not pity," Isabella shot back, her voice shaking. "It's family. I have the means to help, so why shouldn't I? I want to save the farm—our family's legacy!"

Vincenzo's fists clenched at his sides. "When have you cared about family legacy? You think money fixes everything? You left us, Isabella- you are not family. You left us to scrape by, and now you want to play savior? No. We don't want your dirty American dollars."

Maria's voice cut through the tension, firm and commanding. "Enough, Vincenzo. This is my house, and I won't have you speaking to her that way."

But Isabella had already risen, her expression crumbling. "It's okay, Maria. I understand. Thank you for your hospitality, but I think it's time for me to go."

Roberto stood and followed her out, guiding her down the path toward the sea. As they walked into the cool night air, Isabella felt the tears she'd been holding back finally spill over. They walked in silence, tears quietly falling from her cheeks. When they reached the sand, she fell to her knees, her sobs breaking the stillness.

Roberto knelt beside her, pulling her into his arms. "It's okay," he murmured, stroking her back.

As she sank into his embrace, Isabella let the last of her tears fall, her sobs softening into the quiet lapping of the waves.

28

Angela arrived in Villa Montana on a bright and serene May morning. She paused at the bottom of the village, taking in the stunning scene before her: the quaint houses and a tiny church, all nestled against the mountainside, overlooking the vast landscape below. The winding roads leading there had been treacherous, and the little Vespa she rented the day before had barely kept her steady. Now, she hoped for the quiet charm of the village to offer her some relief.

She had no idea where her mother's farm was, or even if she would be there. Turning up unannounced didn't seem like a wise idea—there were too many unknowns, too many variables. Angela was hoping for a warm, welcoming introduction to her long-lost family, not an awkward, uninvited confrontation. She wanted to meet them on her own terms, at least for the first time.

As she made her way up the steep hill toward the piazza, she noticed the curious gazes of the locals. In a village so small, she imagined that everyone knew everyone else, and a stranger was bound to stand out. Angela parked her Vespa and walked toward a cozy café at the edge of the square. She was parched, her throat dry from the journey, and the heat of the day had caught her by surprise. A cold drink and an ice-cream seemed like just the cure.

She took a seat outside, allowing herself a moment to take in the view. She couldn't help but be mesmerized by the beauty of the place. The village was like something out of a dream—Italian architecture winding through narrow cobbled streets, the sea below shimmering in the sunlight. The view was more stunning than any postcard she'd seen. How had her mother kept this hidden from her for so long?

Angela watched the villagers going about their daily lives, and she couldn't help but contrast it with the frantic, impersonal pace of New York. Here, there was an ease to the flow of life—people wandered, greeted one another with smiles, and paused for casual conversations. Everyone seemed connected, as if the village was one big extended family. It was warm, familiar, welcoming.

A waiter approached with a friendly smile. "Buongiorno, Senorina. What can I do for you? I haven't seen you around before."

Angela smiled back, introducing herself. The waiter chuckled, his eyes lighting up. "Ah, I see it now! You must be Isabella's daughter. You look just like her."

Angela blinked, taken aback. "You know my mother?"

He laughed heartily, shaking her hand. "Of course! Everyone knows everyone here—it's a very small place."

Angela was still in shock, but she gathered her thoughts. "Do you know where my mother is staying? I need to find her."

The waiter's smile widened. "You're in luck! She's staying with Roberto Lombardo—just down that little road over there, the fifth house on the left."

Angela could hardly believe how easily she had found her mother. After searching for Jay for so long, she had thought finding her mother would be a little harder. She finished her drink and ice-cream, chatted briefly with the waiter, then thanked him and set off in the direction he had pointed. As she walked toward the tall townhouse, curiosity bubbled inside her. Who was Roberto? There was so much about her mother's past, about her Sicilian family, that Angela didn't know. This village, these people, felt like a mystery and a whole new world for her. The excitement of what lay ahead stirred in her chest. She couldn't wait to meet the family she never knew, and for the first time in a long while, she felt a sense of adventure. Perhaps this journey would offer her the escape she needed—one that would help take her mind off Jay and everything she'd left behind.

29

The morning after the confrontation, Roberto knocked gently on Isabella's door before stepping inside, carrying a cup of steaming coffee. He froze mid-step when he saw her suitcase open on the bed, half-filled with her belongings.

"What are you doing? Leaving already?" He placed the coffee on the bedside table and perched at the end of the bed, moving her case aside.

Isabella folded another blouse and laid it carefully in the suitcase. "I need to go, Roberto. You heard them—they don't want me here. It's too late. I tried, but there's no point. My mamma and Vincenzo will never forgive me."

Roberto sighed deeply, leaning back on his hands. "Come on, Isabella. This isn't the girl I remember. Isabella Verona wouldn't give up that easily. I know you can win them over." He hesitated before adding, "Let me help you."

Isabella paused mid-fold, turning to face him, her eyes searching his. "Why are you being so nice to me? I've never done anything to help you."

Roberto shrugged, a small, wistful smile playing on his lips. "That's not how I operate. I once knew you well. We grew up together, remember? I always thought we were alike in many ways. But you—you were always braver. You had the guts to go after what you wanted, even if it meant leaving everything behind."

She frowned slightly, confused. "Alike? How?"

"I know what it feels like to be misunderstood," he admitted. "To want something different than what everyone expects, to not quite fit the mold. I write and paint, Isabella. All those landscapes you see on the walls downstairs? They're mine."

Her eyes widened in surprise. "Really? They're beautiful. I think I remember your stories too... I loved them. They were the only entertainment we had."

They shared a soft laugh, the memory of their childhood bringing a fleeting warmth to the moment. But the gravity of their conversation soon sobered them again.

"My family never wanted me to be creative," Roberto continued. "They wanted me here, working the farm. I tried to chase my dreams. I went to Rome for a few years—painted, got a few stories published in a magazine. But when Papà fell ill, the guilt became too much. The family needed me, so I came back."

Isabella reached out, her hand resting lightly on his shoulder. "I didn't know that. I'm so sorry, Roberto."

He shook his head. "It was my choice in the end." His gaze dropped to the floor, his voice growing softer. "You know, in a way, I was relieved when you left."

Her face looked confused. "Relieved?"

"I'll never forget when we found out you were promised to Vincenzo. The look on your face—it was a picture. You were only fifteen, but you were furious. The thought of marrying him filled you with dread, and I didn't blame you."

"I was so angry, I dreaded my 16th birthday because of it!" Isabella admitted, her voice barely above a whisper.

Roberto let out a bitter chuckle. "I was jealous. I didn't want my brother to marry you, either. Watching you marry him... It would have destroyed me. So, selfishly, when you left, I was relieved. I was devastated, but I couldn't bear the thought of seeing you with him."

The words hung between them, heavy with years of unspoken emotions. Roberto stood and moved closer, his voice steady but his eyes vulnerable. "The truth is, I was in love with you, Isabella. And I've carried that with me all these years."

Isabella's knees felt weak as the weight of his confession sank in. She turned away, staring out the window as though the rolling hills could offer some kind of clarity.

"Roberto, you don't know me anymore," she murmured. "I've made so many mistakes. My husband hated me. I wasn't a very good mother. I'm not the sweet girl you once knew."

Roberto stepped forward, gently placing a hand on her arm to turn her toward him. "You're wrong," he said firmly. "I do know you. I know about Marco. I know about the son you gave away. I've followed your life from afar, Isabella. I kept up with the New York papers and all the gossip columns, hoping to see your name, to know what you were up to."

She stared at him, stunned.

"I always believed I'd see you again," he continued, his voice breaking slightly. "I hoped, anyway. And these past weeks we've spent together, I've seen glimpses of that girl I loved. The girl who believed in my silly stories and pushed me to dream bigger. She's still in there, Isabella. My friend. My..."

His words faltered, and without thinking, he closed the distance between them. His lips met hers, soft and warm, carrying years of heartache and unspoken love. For a moment, Isabella melted into his embrace, her body aching with the realization of all she had missed.

When they finally pulled apart, Roberto looked into her tear-filled eyes. "Please don't leave again. Stay. We can make this better—together."

Isabella turned back to the window, her emotions warring within her. She touched the glass lightly, her voice barely audible. "I don't know if I deserve that kind of love, Roberto."

He stepped behind her, his voice steady and full of conviction. "You do. You've spent your life running, Isabella. Maybe it's time to stop."

And in that moment, a sense of relief washed over her. She had just felt what it was like to truly feel love from a man—something she had so desperately wanted from Marco and Daniel. And here it was, crashing into her so suddenly and intensely that it took her breath away. She couldn't let this slip through her fingers—not this time. As Isabella stood there, gazing into his longing green eyes, a sense of certainty washed over her—she couldn't leave now. She knew she had to stay. Just as she reached out and took Roberto's hand in hers, a sharp, unexpected knock echoed through the room.

30

Angela knocked on the green door, her breath quickened with anticipation. At first, there was no answer, so she tried again, the sound of her knuckles echoing in the still air. She shifted nervously, eager yet apprehensive about seeing her mother again. Finally, the sound of footsteps grew louder, and the door creaked open to reveal a tall, broad-shouldered man with piercing green eyes and dark, unruly hair.

For a moment, he simply stared, his expression a mix of shock and recognition, before breaking into a wide, warm grin. "You... you look just like your mother," he said, his voice tinged with amazement. Without warning, he pulled Angela into a firm embrace. She stiffened, awkwardly patting his back, unsure of who this stranger was.

"Sorry, I should introduce myself," he said, stepping back and extending a hand. "I'm Roberto, an old friend of your mother's."

Angela smiled politely as she shook his hand. "Lovely to meet you. I'm Angela."

He grinned again, then called over his shoulder, "Isabella, come down! You have a visitor!"

Angela heard quick, uneven footsteps on the stairs. When her mother appeared, her face pale and her eyes red-rimmed, she froze at the sight of her daughter.

"Surprise," Angela said softly, smiling through the sudden lump in her throat.

Isabella's expression crumpled as she rushed forward and enveloped Angela in a hug so tight it felt like she was trying to anchor herself. "Are you okay, Mother? What's wrong?" Angela whispered, sensing the raw emotion radiating from her mother.

Roberto chuckled awkwardly, trying to lighten the mood. "Careful, Isabella. You're going to squeeze the poor girl to death!"

Reluctantly, Isabella released her and kissed her forehead. "I'm just so happy to see you, Angela. You don't know how much."

Roberto gestured toward the staircase. "Come on, let's go up to the roof terrace. You can take in the view while we chat."

As they settled on the terrace, Angela couldn't help but marvel at the breathtaking sight of the sparkling sea and the quaint village below. It was like something out of a dream.

"It's beautiful, isn't it?" Isabella said, her voice softer now. "I've spent most of my time here, just staring out at that view, thinking."

"It's incredible," Angela said, but her tone turned concerned. "Are you sure you're okay, Mother? You seem... sad."

Isabella sighed heavily and glanced at Roberto. He gave her a small nod and excused himself to fetch coffee, leaving the two women alone. Isabella took a deep breath and began to explain, recounting her arrival in the village, her estranged mother's refusal to see her, and the tense confrontation with Vincenzo.

"But, Mother, you can't leave now," Angela said firmly, her determination cutting through the tension.

"That's what I've been telling her," Roberto said as he returned with a tray of coffee. He set it down and joined them. "She can't give up now."

Angela nodded, her voice steady and full of conviction. "You have to stay, Mother. You need to show them you're serious about rebuilding these relationships. We can help you. We'll work on the farm, do whatever needs to be done. Maybe we can even investigate this corporation that's threatening the land and find a legal way to stop them. But leaving now? That's not the answer."

Isabella's eyes filled with tears as she looked at her daughter. "You've always been so wise, Angela. The empathetic one in the family. If anyone knows how to fix this, it's you."

Roberto gave a hearty laugh. "She's definitely her mother's daughter. That fire... I remember it well."

Isabella stood abruptly, a newfound resolve in her posture. "You're both right. I can't run away. I've made mistakes, but I can make amends. If they won't accept my financial help, then I'll find another way. Maybe a fundraiser, something that feels like their idea, to help save the farm. I can do this."

"Yes!" Angela said, practically bouncing on her feet. "Mother, you were always amazing at organizing events. We've got this!"

Roberto raised a hand, a smile tugging at his lips. "One step at a time, ladies. Let's start with the land and earning their trust. Then we can think about fundraisers and plans. But whatever you do, make sure Vincenzo thinks it's his idea, or he'll never go for it."

Isabella and Angela exchanged a determined glance. "So, where are the farm clothes? I'm ready to start now," Angela said with a grin.

Isabella blinked, momentarily stunned. "You're serious? We're actually going to do this?"

"Of course," Angela said. "We're in this together."

Roberto's laughter echoed across the terrace. "Don't worry, Isabella. It's like riding a bike—you'll remember. I'll grab some old clothes for you both, we'll just have to make do for now."

As the three of them descended the stairs, a new sense of purpose filled the air. They were ready to face whatever challenges lay ahead, together

31

Angela, Roberto, and Isabella arrived at the farm every morning at 6 a.m. for an entire month. The mornings were cool, with dew still clinging to the fields, but by midday, the sun bore down relentlessly, turning the land into a furnace. From the start, Vincenzo and Caterina barely acknowledged their presence. Vincenzo's lingering resentment over Isabella's offer of money was palpable, his curt nods and sidelong glares speaking volumes. Roberto, once Vincenzo's closest ally, was now regarded with suspicion for siding with Isabella. Despite this, the three newcomers refused to give up. They worked tirelessly, shoulders to the grindstone, until the sun dipped below the horizon.

Maria, on the other hand, welcomed their efforts. She'd often bring them snacks and cool lemonade when the sun became unbearable, just as she used to when they were younger. Over time, Maria grew fond of Angela, delighting in her stories about life in New York and her relationship with Jay. Angela, in turn, cherished Maria's wisdom and warmth but couldn't help but feel a pang of sadness whenever Caterina turned her back or ignored her attempts to connect. Sometimes, Angela would catch her grandmother watching from a window, her expression unreadable, but as soon as their eyes met, Caterina would retreat, leaving Angela with a hollow ache.

Roberto remained a constant presence, teaching them about the farm's daily operations with patience and humor. Angela, naturally drawn to caring for the animals, embraced the experience wholeheartedly. She applied what she'd learned in her studies, tending to the sick livestock with tenderness and ingenuity. Each day, her conviction grew stronger—this was what she wanted for her future.

Working alongside her mother also felt transformative. For the first time, they weren't just mother and daughter—they were partners. They laughed, teased each other, and bonded in ways Angela had only dreamed of. Isabella, too, seemed lighter, freer, especially in Roberto's company. He brought out a playful side of her, regaling them with funny stories from their childhood and inventing silly rhymes about the villagers. Angela often caught fleeting glances and soft smiles between the two, evidence of a blossoming affection that filled her heart with hope.

One particularly hot June day, Vincenzo finally extended an olive branch. He invited them to join the family for lunch under the pergola, the scent of fresh basil and tomatoes wafting through the air. As they ate, Vincenzo shared his worries.

"The crops are struggling," he admitted, his voice heavy with defeat. "The animals are getting sick, and nothing we've tried has worked. Last week, Leonardo Manucci from Gruppo di Vita came by again. He said the bank's ready to foreclose next month and made another offer to buy the farm directly to avoid the process."

"And what did you say?" Isabella asked, though she already knew the answer.

"I told him no," Vincenzo said firmly. "But it won't matter if the bank moves ahead."

"How much do you owe?" Isabella pressed.

When Vincenzo named the amount, the table fell silent. It was staggering. Isabella's mind raced, knowing her fortune could easily erase the debt, but offering money again would only worsen the rift.

Angela spoke up, her voice steady. "I'm going to call my father. Big corporations are his expertise, and he can help us dig into Gruppo di Vita. Maybe there's a way to fight back."

Over the next couple weeks, Angela was constantly on the phone with Daniel, piecing together information about the company. Meanwhile, the farm's troubles worsened. The animals grew sicker, and some began to die. One morning, the family gathered around the large farm table, the air thick with tension and worry.

"This is your fault!" Vincenzo shouted, pointing at Isabella. "Ever since you arrived, everything's gone wrong. You've cursed us!"

"Enough!" Roberto snapped, rising from his seat. "Isabella has done nothing but help since she got here. You've refused her at every turn!"

"Of course, you'd defend her," Vincenzo sneered. "You're so blinded by her that you can't see straight. She'll chew you up and spit you out, just like she did with this family and her husband. You're wasting your time. Do you ever think a rich woman like her would look at a poor artist like you?"

Roberto lunged, landing a punch square on Vincenzo's jaw. Vincenzo retaliated, shoving him hard against the wall.

"Stop it!" Maria screamed, her voice cutting through the chaos. "Enough of this! We have bigger problems than you two fighting like children."

Angela stood, her voice steady but urgent. "Maria's right. We need to stop tearing each other apart and start working together. The way you've behaved towards my mother is unacceptable. We're family, and if we want to save this farm, we need to act like it. My mother isn't the enemy—Gruppo di Vita is. Let's focus on that. I've already spoken to my father, and my sister Bianca, who's a lawyer. They are coming to help. I've also called my college tutor, Michael Fitzpatrick. He's a vet and one of the best in his field. If anyone can figure out what's happening to the animals, it's him. They are all catching the next flight out here. Please, let's move forward as a team."

The room fell silent as Angela finished, her words hanging in the air. Slowly, Caterina began to sob. She stood and crossed the room to Angela, her weathered hands trembling as she cupped her granddaughter's face.

"You remind me so much of your grandfather," she said through tears. "He was always the one to bring us together, to make us see sense. I'm sorry I've been so cold towards you. I've carried so much pain for so long, but you're right—it's time to let it go. If we want to save the farm, we need to put all of this behind us."

Turning to Isabella, Caterina pulled them both into a tight embrace. "Welcome home, Isabella. I've missed you, I am sorry."

tears fell freely as she hugged her mother and daughter, relief washing over her like a wave.

From across the room, Vincenzo sighed, his anger melting into resignation. "Angela is right," he muttered. "We'll never win this fight if we don't stand together."

"Then it's settled," Roberto said, his voice firm but kind. "We'll face this as a family."

Angela smiled, her mind swelling with hope. "We won't let them take this farm. Not now, not ever."

The two families nodded in unison, a newfound determination settling over them like armor. Together, they would fight for their homes and for each other.

32

Michael arrived the next day on the morning flight. Angela, Isabella, and Roberto went to the airport to pick him up. As he emerged from the Arrivals gate, Angela ran toward him with delight, giving him the biggest hug. Relief and joy surged through her as she knew Michael would help get to the bottom of the animal sickness. She couldn't wait to see him in action, observing and learning from his expertise.

Angela eagerly grabbed his luggage and brought him over to meet her mother. Michael, without hesitation, enveloped Isabella in a warm and sincere embrace. Isabella was taken by surprise, but instantly, a sense of calm and trust settled over her- his welcoming energy was contagious. "It is so wonderful to finally meet you, Mrs. Hastings. Angela has told me so much about you," Michael said warmly.

Isabella smiled at the tall man before her, a stranger yet somehow familiar and clearly someone who had made a significant impact on Angela's life. "Please, call me Isabella. The pleasure is all mine. We're so grateful for you coming all this way to help us. Angela speaks so highly of you, and I can't thank you enough for supporting her with her studies."

Angela squealed with excitement, certain Michael would love everyone at the farm and be a hero to them all. She introduced Roberto, and soon they were on their way back.

Once at the farm, Michael wasted no time. After warm introductions to both families, he went straight out onto the land to examine the animals. Despite his exhaustion from the red-eye flight, he was determined not to lose a moment in finding answers. Angela stayed by his side every second, helping, taking notes, and observing him closely. Michael spoke his thoughts aloud as he worked, turning each moment into a teaching opportunity for Angela.

"It can't be bacterial or viral. It just doesn't add up," he muttered, frowning as he examined the animals. Angela had provided detailed timelines of the symptoms, but Michael noted inconsistencies. Some animals were perfectly healthy, while others were gravely ill or dying. It didn't make sense.

He worked tirelessly until nightfall, collecting samples and running tests until he could barely stand. As the sun set, Maria called them both for dinner. The evenings had grown warmer, and under the sprawling pergola, a massive wooden table had been set for a feast. Twinkling string lights hung overhead, casting a soft, golden glow that complemented the fiery hues of the setting sun. The table was laden with dishes, a tapestry of flavors and colors. Freshly baked bread rested in wicker baskets, olive oil gleaming in little bowls beside it. Platters of grilled vegetables, steaming pasta dishes, vibrant salads, and roasted meats filled every inch of the table. The aroma of garlic, basil, and rosemary mingled with the salty breeze from the nearby sea.

Franco, Marla and Caterina had spent the entire day preparing the meal, a heartfelt gesture of gratitude for Michael's arrival. Glasses of deep red wine were passed around, and the chatter of voices, laughter, and the occasional clink of utensils created a symphony of warmth and togetherness.

Michael sat opposite Isabella and Roberto, his weariness momentarily forgotten as he soaked in the scene before him. He could feel the energy of love and connection radiating from the families gathered around the table. Turning to Angela, he smiled through the exhaustion, his eyes glistening. "Am I dreaming?" he laughed softly. "Isn't this perfect? One big family, all eating together as the sun sets over the sea. It's like something out of a fairytale."

Angela's face lit up as she gazed at him. "I know what you mean. This past month has been an eye-opener for me too. This is what I always longed for as a child—a big, warm family, chaotic with laughter and debates. No one standing on ceremony with polite conversations, just real, raw emotions filled with love and acceptance. These two families are definitely that. And I love it. I've never seen my mum like this either. My family was quite the opposite. It's so refreshing to see her like this."

They both paused to take in the scene: the golden light filtering through the pergola, the laughter ringing out as stories were shared, the vibrant dishes being passed around with eager hands. Michael's gaze softened as he looked across the table. "It was just me, my mom, and dad growing up. We used to eat at the kitchen table because my mom said there wasn't any point in setting the dining room for just three people."

Angela gave him a comforting smile. "I can understand that. But wouldn't it be wonderful if your parents could experience something like this? A big, loud, loving family meal?"

Michael's expression shifted, a flicker of sadness passing over his face. "My mom passed away just over a year ago," he said quietly.

Angela's eyes widened, and she reached out to touch his arm. "Oh, Michael, I'm so sorry for your loss."

He gave her a small, appreciative smile. "Thank you. It's been tough, but it's also made me realize how much I want something like this for my future. That's why I've told Shanika I want us to have a big family one day."

Angela squeezed his hand, a soft glow spread through her at his words. "Wouldn't that be perfect?"

As the stars began to twinkle in the deepening sky, the families lingered at the table, savoring the food, the wine, and the company. The night felt endless, filled with warmth and belonging. For Angela and Michael, it was a moment to treasure, a reminder of the beauty in shared experiences and the power of connection.

Just as the meal was coming to an end, rustling came from one of the bushes at the edge of the property. Two voices called out, "Hello, are you back here?" The group turned toward the sound, and out of the darkness, two figures emerged into the light of the pergola. It was Daniel and Bianca.

"We've been knocking on the door, but it's clear you're all having too much fun out here to hear us," Daniel said with a chuckle.

Everyone laughed, rising from their seats to greet the unexpected arrivals. "Why didn't you tell us you were coming tonight, Father? We could have picked you up," Angela said as she embraced her father, feeling the warmth of his familiar presence.

Daniel pulled her into a loving hug, his voice full of affection. Bianca followed, wrapping her arms around Angela in a rare display of warmth. The hug was the longest and most heartfelt Angela had ever received from her usually aloof sister.

"We didn't want to put anyone out," Daniel explained. "We took the jet and arranged for a car to bring us here. Everything was very smooth."

"I'm so pleased you're both here," Angela said, her voice brimming with happiness.

Isabella rose to her feet, a mix of surprise and delight on her face as she approached her ex-husband. She gave Daniel a welcoming embrace and pressed a kiss to Bianca's cheeks. "It's wonderful to see you both. Come, sit down."

She introduced them to everyone gathered at the table, and Maria quickly called out for more wine and bread. "Please, sit. You must both be starving," Maria said, bustling toward the kitchen with Franco to bring out more food.

What had felt like the winding down of the evening now had a new burst of energy. Fresh plates of food were brought to the table, and wine glasses were filled once more.

Laughter and chatter filled the air as the families fussed over their new guests, sharing stories and updates.

Angela couldn't help but notice how different Bianca seemed. The once standoffish and guarded sister now looked relaxed and at ease, engaging warmly with both families. She laughed easily and leaned in to listen as the Lombardos and Veronas filled her and Daniel in on the challenges and pressures from Gruppo di Vita. Bianca's sharp legal mind was already at work, outlining strategies to counteract the situation. Daniel, ever the connector, shared insights from local business leaders he'd spoken to, warning them of the company, offering a sense of hope and direction.

Angela watched it all with a sense of awe and contentment. This was what she had always dreamed of—family coming together, not just in proximity but in purpose and unity. The air was alive with energy and the kind of camaraderie that made the world feel a little less daunting.

As Angela turned to talk to Michael about sharing their findings with the families, she noticed him slumped in his chair, his head tilted to the side, fast asleep. The long day had caught up to him, and exhaustion had finally won.

Smiling, Angela gently tapped his shoulder. "Come on," she whispered. "I'll show you to your room."

Michael stirred, blinking at her with a sleepy grin. She helped him up, steadying him as they walked toward the old farmhouse. The warmth of the evening followed them, and Angela felt a deep sense of peace knowing they were surrounded by so much love and support.

33

The next few days were a whirlwind. Bianca and Daniel spent hours camped out at the farmhouse dining table, pouring over finances, contracts, and documents related to Gruppo di Vita. Angela dipped in and out of the discussions but spent most of her time with Michael, helping him care for the animals. Michael had sent samples to the lab in the nearest town and called them frequently to check on the results.

"Things move a bit slower here, unfortunately," Angela teased with a small smile.

Isabella and Roberto spent their days working together in the fields or cleaning out the animal pens alongside Angela and Michael. Whenever they had a chance, they would sneak off for walks through the rolling countryside or refreshing swims in the wild sea. Isabella had never felt so alive. Her romance with Roberto deepened with every shared moment, but they kept it as private as possible. Although Vincenzo was now married and living his own life, it was clear he hadn't fully let go of the past, and the revelation of Roberto and Isabella's relationship would undoubtedly stir old animosities.

"Vincenzo always gloated about you being promised to him," Roberto admitted one afternoon as they lay in the long grass overlooking the sea. "He knew how much I cared about you, even back then. It ate me up, thinking you were to be married."

Isabella reached for his hand, entwining her fingers with his. "And now?" she whispered, her voice trembling with emotion.

Roberto turned to her, his expression soft yet resolute. "Now, I feel like the luckiest man alive. You came back to me, Isabella. This is our chance to start fresh, to build the life we were always meant to have."

He kissed her deeply, and as Isabella pulled away, her eyes sparkled with both joy and determination. "For the first time in my life, I feel genuinely excited about the future. I want to be better—for myself, for you, for my girls, and for this farm. Together, I know we can do this."

Roberto smiled, brushing a stray strand of hair from her face. "You've given me the confidence to pursue my dreams, and I'll support you with yours. Whatever happens with the farm, we'll face it together."

Later that afternoon, as everyone rested during the siesta, Isabella found herself drawn to a familiar spot—a weathered bench nestled under a large tree. It was the same bench where she had once sat with her father, listening to his stories about life in the markets of Milan before the war. She closed her eyes, her heart heavy with memories. She had come full circle—back where it had all began all those years ago.

"Papa, I miss you," she murmured. "I'm sorry I let you down, but I promise I'll make things right."

A soft hand on her shoulder startled her. Turning, she saw Daniel standing behind her, his expression filled with concern. "Are you okay, Iz?" he asked gently.

Isabella gestured for him to sit beside her, wiping a tear from her cheek. "I was just thinking about my father," she admitted. "I feel like I've failed him. I wasn't a good wife, and I wasn't the mother our children deserved."

Daniel sighed, his voice tinged with regret. "We both made mistakes, Isabella. Our marriage wasn't what it should have been, and we let that affect our kids. Angela shouldn't have had to go through everything she did to wake us up. But she's stronger now. Happier. And I think we're all learning how to be better."

Isabella nodded, fresh tears spilling down her cheeks. "She's been a light in the darkness. I just wish things had worked out with Jay. It's going to be so hard for her to move on while he's still in her life."

Daniel frowned. "Susie hasn't heard from him in a while. I think she's starting to get worried and I don't want to tell Angela otherwise she'll worry too. She seems so happy here, I don't want to ruin it for her. He sends the occasional postcard, but he's vague about what he's doing or how he's feeling. I just hope he comes home soon."

"Poor Angela," Isabella murmured. "At least she has Michael, he's been her rock. He's been incredible—not just with the farm but with her studies too. She looks up to him so much."

Daniel hesitated. "He's been great, no question. But something about him feels oddly familiar to me, and I can't put my finger on it. Still, hearing Angela call him a father figure—" He paused, his voice thick with emotion. "It stings, but I know I deserve that. I wasn't there for her the way I should have been. I'm trying to change that now."

They sat in silence for a few moments before Daniel stood and turned to Isabella, his expression earnest. "I've seen how Roberto looks at you—and how you look at him. I've never seen you like this. It's refreshing, Iz. You deserve to be happy. Let go of the guilt and give yourself a chance."

Isabella's tears flowed freely as she reached for Daniel's hand. "Thank you. Being here has helped me heal. I've realized how much of myself I lost after Marco—after giving up my son. But I'm starting to feel whole again. Roberto has shown me what love really means. I have finally discovered, only now, that healing and self-acceptance is where love begins—for myself and for others."

Daniel pulled her into a gentle hug, pressing a kiss to the top of her head. "Absolutely. The past is behind us, Isabella. It's time to look forward—to build something new, for ourselves and for our children."

Hand in hand, they walked back to the farmhouse, ready to face whatever challenges lay ahead as a united family.

34

A few days later, on a boiling summers morning, Michael, Angela, and Roberto spent time in the field, where they were teaching Angela how to milk the cows. The air was thick with heat, laughter, and the earthy smells of the farm. Angela giggled as she struggled to get the hang of it, the milk spraying comically across her face and onto her clothes. The others roared with laughter, the light-hearted chaos bonding them even more.

Michael wiped his brow, his face glowing with joy. "Isn't this perfect? The smells of this place, the sun beating down— there's something about it that feels like home. Being here definitely confirms I have Italian blood in me."

Angela stopped mid-laugh, tilting her head in confusion. "What do you mean, Italian? You said your parents were true Canadians. That's where you grew up, right?"

Michael hesitated, his smile faltering for a moment. "Yes, you're right. I am Canadian. I actually spent the first year of my life in New York, though. Then my mother had a breakdown, and we moved to Canada to live with my grandmother until she got better."

Angela blinked, sensing there was more to the story. "I didn't know that, sorry."

Michael nodded, his expression shifting to one of deep thought. "When my mom passed away last year, it was really hard on my dad. He couldn't do much of anything, and he needed to sell our house. It was too big for one man. I helped him clear out the attic. That's when I found something... unexpected." His voice dropped slightly, the weight of his words hanging in the air.

The laughter died down as everyone instinctively turned to Michael, sensing the shift in tone. Even the cows seemed to settle, as though they, too, were listening.

"There was a stack of old magazines," Michael continued, glancing at Isabella with a hint of nervousness. "Many of them had you in them, Mrs. Hastings. I think my mum must have been a fan. But underneath that stack, I found a folder—a folder full of paperwork. Most of it was blacked out, though, like someone didn't want me to read it. At the back of the folder, I discovered something that turned my world upside down," Michael said, his voice trembling as he paused to steady himself. He swallowed hard before continuing, his words slow and deliberate. "It was an adoption certificate... and my name was on it." Angela's heart dropped into her stomach as her eyes darted to her mother. Isabella's face had gone pale, her hands trembling slightly. The oppressive heat of the day seemed to intensify as the weight of Michael's revelation settled over them.

"Could you read anything else on the paperwork?" Angela asked, her voice barely above a whisper.

Michael stroked the cow next to him, his movements slow and deliberate as though grounding himself. "Not much," he admitted. "But I could make out a few details. Both of my birth parents were Italian, and my birth mother was only sixteen when she had me." He paused, his voice thick with emotion. "I've never told anyone about this except Shanika. Not even my dad. I didn't want to hurt him. But coming here—being here with all of you—it feels different. Peaceful. Like I'm where I'm supposed to be."

The silence that followed was deafening. Angela's gaze flickered between Michael and her mother, whose face was now ashen, her chest rising and falling rapidly. Isabella suddenly swayed, and before anyone could react, she collapsed to the ground.

"Mother!" Angela cried, rushing to her side. Roberto knelt beside her, his face etched with concern. Isabella's eyes fluttered open, but she seemed dazed, her lips trembling.

Michael knelt down as well, his brow knotted in confusion. "Mrs. Hastings, are you okay? What's wrong? Are you hurt?"

Isabella reached out, her fingers brushing Michael's arm as though confirming he was real. Her voice was barely audible. "Your eyes... your smile... I knew I had seen them before. Michael, when is your birthday?"

Michael froze, his confusion deepening. "What does that have to do with—"

"Please," Isabella interrupted, her voice urgent. "Tell me." He hesitated, glancing at Angela and Roberto, who were both watching with wide, anxious eyes. "It's August 8th, 1966," he finally said.

The moment the words left his mouth, Isabella let out a guttural cry, a sound so raw it seemed to tear through the very fabric of the moment. She stumbled to her feet, clutching her stomach as though she had been physically struck. "Oh, Dio mio..." she whispered, tears streaming down her face. She looked at Michael, her eyes filled with a mixture of anguish and hope. "Michael, I am so sorry. Please forgive me. Please know that I have thought of you every single day of my life."

Michael staggered back, his face pale. "What are you saying? What do you...?" He couldn't finish the sentence, his voice breaking.

Isabella stepped closer, her hands trembling as she reached for his. "When I was sixteen, I arrived in New York. I was young and naive, with nothing but dreams and a desperate hope for a better life. I met a man—a man I thought I loved. But when I found out I was pregnant, a week later he was arrested and put in jail. I had nothing. No proper family, no money, no support. The nuns at St. Nicholas took me in. They cared for me until I gave birth to a beautiful baby boy on August 8th, 1966, just a month before my seventeenth birthday."

Angela's hand flew to her mouth as tears streamed down her face. She looked at Michael, then back at her mother, the pieces of the puzzle falling into place with horrifying clarity.

Isabella's voice cracked as she continued. "I wanted to give you more than I could offer. I wanted you to have a life full of opportunities and love. So I made the hardest decision of my life. I gave you up. And I have regretted it every single day since. I tried finding you, I searched everywhere and every time I failed. I had to come to terms with the fact I would never know who you were. But you're here now. You came back to me."

Michael's legs gave out beneath him, and Roberto caught him, holding him steady as he struggled to process what he had just heard. "You're saying... you're my... my mother?"

Isabella nodded, tears streaming freely down her face. "Yes, Michael. There are too many coincidences. And you have Marco's tall physique, his dark hair and his eyes but my father's kind smile. You must be my son."

For a moment, no one moved. Then, as though something inside him broke free, Michael stepped forward and pulled Isabella into his arms. They sank to their knees together, holding each other tightly as sobs wracked their bodies. Angela knelt beside them, wrapping her arms around both of them, her own tears falling like rain. She felt as though this wasn't real, as though she was in a dream. She couldn't even begin to process what had just happened. All the time they had spent together, their deep and instant connection, the bond she couldn't explain, now made sense in the most unimaginable way. He wasn't just Michael anymore. He was her brother. He always had been.

Roberto joined them, his strong arms encircling them all, offering silent support. The four of them knelt there in the field, a tangled mess of emotions, as the weight of the past gave way to the hope of a new beginning.

35

The next few days passed in a haze for Angela. Once the news about Michael reached the entire family, the emotions poured out in waves. Tears were shed freely as they came together to welcome him into their lives. Everyone was in a state of shock, but there was an overwhelming sense of joy too. Isabella, unable to contain her relief, stayed glued to Michael's side, as if afraid he might disappear again, trying to make up for all those lost years.

Their focus shifted entirely from the turmoil at the farm to Michael's story. For hours, they gathered around the long wooden table, hanging on every word as Michael recounted his life, his upbringing, and his adoptive parents. Isabella clung to the details, her heart equal parts aching and comforted.

"I'm so glad," she said, her voice trembling, "that you had a stable, loving home. It sounds like they gave you the kind of life I always dreamed you'd have."

Michael smiled warmly, but his expression was tinged with sadness. "They did. I was lucky. They gave me everything—opportunity, love, stability. But even then, there was always this... sense of being different, like I didn't quite fit."

He paused, his dark eyes meeting Isabella's. "It explains a lot, actually. That unexplainable pull I felt toward Angela when I first met her. I told Shanika about it—how I couldn't put my finger on why I was so invested in her potential. It was like something bigger than me was guiding me, telling me I needed to help her."

The revelation hit Angela like a wave, leaving her both awed and unsettled. It was as if fate had been orchestrating their lives all along, pulling invisible strings to bring them together.

Michael went on, his tone turning introspective. "I always wondered why I looked so different from my family. My parents were both small, fair-haired, and light-eyed. Meanwhile, I was this tall, dark-featured kid. My dad—he's a doctor—used to joke about recessive genetics, but it never really satisfied me."

After a few days of talking and crying, Michael decided it was time to confront his father. He needed answers, even though he knew it would be painful for both of them. He paced the room, phone in hand, before finally dialing the number. The call lasted hours, and when Michael returned, he looked emotionally drained.

"My dad... he was in bits," Michael said, his voice thick with emotion. "It took him at least twenty minutes to stop crying before he could even speak. He told me how he and my mom tried for years to have children, but it never happened for them. Then, one day, they got a call from a convent—a baby boy was about to be born, and they were asked if they wanted to adopt him. He said they felt like the luckiest people in the world."

Michael swallowed hard, his voice trembling. "But my mom... she struggled. She couldn't come to terms with the fact that I wasn't biologically hers. She started faking a pregnancy so no one would know I was adopted. When I was born, she made sure my dad collected every document from the convent and keep anything that could trace my existence back to my biological family.

"For a while, they were happy. But then, one day, she saw Isabella in a magazine. Then on billboards. Everywhere she turned, it was like Isabella was haunting her. My dad said she became obsessed, convinced it was some kind of punishment. She started buying every magazine with Isabella in it, and eventually... she had a breakdown. One day, she took the adoption papers and blacked out nearly every detail about my biological family. Then my dad applied for a job in Toronto, and we moved, hoping to escape it all."

The room fell silent. Angela felt a deep sadness for Michael's adoptive mother. She had spent her life terrified, unable to truly enjoy motherhood because of her anxiety and guilt. Isabella, meanwhile, looked devastated.

"All these years," Isabella murmured, her voice barely audible. "I missed you so much. I thought about you every day. And all the while, she was suffering because of me..."

The emotional atmosphere was shattered by a sudden knock at the door. Maria opened it to reveal Leonardo Manucci, flanked by a bank representative holding a thick brown envelope.

The bank manager stepped forward, his tone curt. "We're here to inform you that in two days' time, this farm will be repossessed, and the paperwork to transfer ownership to Gruppo di Vita will be finalized. You must vacate the property by then."

Leonardo smirked, his gaze cold as he added, "I told you this would've been easier if you'd sold it directly to us. Now, you'll leave with nothing."

As the men turned to leave, Vincenzo lunged toward them, fury etched on his face, but Roberto held him back. Daniel took the envelope and began sifting through the documents with Bianca, while Marla and the children broke into tears.

"We can't let this happen," Franco declared, slamming his fist on the table. "There has to be a way!"

Bianca nodded firmly. "We'll go through these papers, find something—anything—to buy us more time."

"Mamma, please," Isabella pleaded. "We can save the farm, we have the money. Or at least let me organize a fundraiser—the village and neighboring towns would help us!"

Catarina shook her head firmly, her tear-streaked face resolute. "No, amore. We do not take charity in this family. If the farm is not meant to be ours, then that is God's will, and we will accept it."

She walked out onto the veranda, leaving the rest of the family in stunned silence.

"We can't give up," Franco said, slamming his fist on the table again. "There has to be a way!"

Just then, the phone rang. Maria answered and called out, "It's for you, Michael."

Michael disappeared into the kitchen. When he returned, he looked drained but determined.

"That was the lab," he announced. "The results are in. The animals weren't sick—they were poisoned."

Gasps echoed around the room.

"Poisoned?" Vincenzo exclaimed. "How? No one else has access to the barn."

The room fell into a heavy silence. Daniel broke it, his voice steady but laced with urgency. "We need to go back to the dates when the animals fell sick and trace who was around the farm at those times. Was there anything unusual, anything at all, that happened just before the sickness started?"

Everyone exchanged glances, their hands on their heads as they tried to rewind the clock. The tension was thick, each person sifting through their memories in a desperate search for answers. Finally, Mario spoke up, his tone determined. "I have the vet call-out receipts. They'll have the dates on them—I'll go check." He rushed off to the study, leaving the rest of the family to sit in uneasy anticipation.

Vincenzo, ever the hothead, was pacing now, muttering accusations under his breath. "It could've been anyone," he grumbled. "The mailman. That drunk who shows up every few weeks, always looking for trouble. Hell, maybe even one of the neighbors who's been jealous of the farm's success."

Marla rolled her eyes. "Vincenzo, be serious. You're grasping at straws."

Before Vincenzo could retort, Mario returned, clutching a folder thick with receipts. He laid them on the table, flipping through them quickly. Marla leaned over to help, scanning the dates and wracking her brain for anything significant. Suddenly, she gasped, her hand flying to her mouth.

"I remember now," she said, her voice trembling with a mix of realization and fear. "It was Leonardo Manucci. He came around the farm the first time, just before the animals got sick. He asked me for a tour. I didn't think much of it—he hadn't told me who he really was yet. But then he came back. I caught him loitering near the barn that second time. When I confronted him, he told me he was making plans for where *his* swimming pool was going to be." Her voice broke, and she shook her head in disbelief. "I thought he was just being a smug idiot, but now... it all makes sense."

Mario quickly dug through a separate pile of letters. "I kept every official offer he gave us when he visited," he said, spreading them out on the table. One by one, they matched up perfectly with the dates of the sickness.

The chatter erupted—everyone speaking at once, their voices a mix of anger, disbelief, and frustration. But it was Daniel who spoke the hard truth. "This isn't enough. No court will take coinciding dates as solid evidence. We need something more concrete—something that proves he was directly responsible for poisoning the animals."

As his words sank in, a heavy silence returned to the room. Vincenzo, who had suddenly been uncharacteristically quiet during the exchange, began to shift awkwardly in his seat. He scratched the back of his head, his eyes darting to Marla and then to Roberto.

"There might be... something," he said finally, his voice hesitant and low. All eyes turned to him, curiosity and suspicion rippling through the room.

"What do you mean?" Roberto asked sharply, his tone edged with irritation.

Vincenzo cleared his throat and adjusted his collar as if the weight of what he was about to confess was suffocating him. His cheeks flushed a deep red. "When Isabella and Angela came to the farm... I didn't trust them," he admitted, his voice barely above a whisper. "I aslo knew Roberto was lying about nothing going on between him and Isabella. And I was angry—still angry about the past. I wanted her out."

The air in the room became electric with tension. Marla's face fell, hurt flickering in her eyes. Roberto's fists clenched at his sides, his jaw tightening. Isabella, sensing a storm brewing, placed a calming hand on Roberto's arm. "Let him finish," she said softly.

Vincenzo exhaled shakily, his gaze fixed on the floor. "So... I installed a nanny cam in the barn. A small CCTV camera. I wanted proof of... well, proof of something, anything, to justify how I felt." He paused, glancing nervously at Marla, whose hurt expression made his voice falter. "I kept the tapes. They go back a couple of months. I never got around to looking at them because... well, after everything calmed down, it just didn't seem important anymore. But they're still there."

The room was utterly still. Marla's face had turned pale, and Roberto looked like he was moments away from an outburst. But Bianca was the first to speak, her voice cutting through the awkward tension like a blade.

"Vincenzo... if those tapes show Leonardo in the barn with poison or doing anything suspicious, that's exactly the proof we need."

The mood in the room shifted almost instantly. What had been a moment of betrayal now shimmered with the faintest glimmer of hope. Daniel stood and clapped Vincenzo on the shoulder. "You might've just saved this farm," he said, his voice firm but not unkind.

The family sprang into action. "Me and Dad will start going through the tapes," Bianca announced, already moving toward Vincenzo's study. "As soon as we have something, we'll call the police. And then, we'll build the strongest case possible to sue this company into the ground. They won't know what hit them."

The room erupted into cheers and hugs. It was the first moment of light after months of despair. But amidst the celebration, Angela stood quietly in the corner, her mind drifting far away.

She thought of Jay. His face filled her mind, his warm smile and steady presence like a balm to her aching soul. Over the past few days, she had tried to push thoughts of him away, knowing she had to focus on her family. But the truth was, she missed him more deeply than she had words for.

Her father noticed her faraway expression and walked over, placing a gentle hand on her shoulder. "Are you alright, Angela?" he asked softly. "Don't worry. We'll get through this. Everything will work out."

Angela sighed, shaking her head. "It's not that, Father. I just... I miss him. I miss Jay. He's always been there for me during times like this. I wish he was here now. His missed out on so much. I know everyone would love him."

Daniel gave her a sympathetic smile and pulled her into a hug. "I know, sweetheart. And I'm sure he's fine. Things will work out—you'll see."

She nodded, but his words couldn't shake the ache in her body. She excused herself and slipped out for a walk, the cool evening air brushing against her skin as she made her way to the beach. Sitting on the warm sand, she closed her eyes, letting the sound of the waves calm her frayed nerves. She imagined herself back in the Hamptons, Jay by her side, holding her hand as they shared stories of their summer adventures.

The memory made her smile, but it was bittersweet. As she lay there, lost in her thoughts, she eventually drifted off to sleep, clinging to the hope that one day, this would be her reality again.

36

For the next 48 hours, hardly anyone slept. The entire family was consumed with tasks—gathering evidence, reviewing tapes, and speaking to the police. It was a race against time to ensure justice was served. After five hours of painstakingly sifting through the nanny cam footage, meticulously watching the barn's comings and goings, the moment they'd all been waiting for arrived.

There he was: Leonardo Manucci, caught red-handed. The footage showed him clutching a distinctive bottle, wearing gloves and a mask, as he poured its contents into the animal feed silo. Not once, but twice. Bianca's triumphant shout echoed through the room. "Bingo!"

Everyone rushed to the screen as she rewound the footage, playing back the incriminating moment. Gasps and exclamations filled the room as the family watched Leonardo's crime unfold before their eyes.

"We've got him!" Daniel exclaimed, the palm of his hand slamming the table with satisfaction.

Bianca and Daniel immediately got to work drafting the necessary paperwork for the authorities. Their faces were set with determination as they prepared the evidence to be delivered to Gruppo di Vita's offices the next morning. The police had already paid the company a visit the day before, and now there would be no doubt about what was coming.

Meanwhile, Daniel managed to secure a temporary extension from the bank, citing the ongoing criminal investigation. For the first time in weeks, hope began to blossom among the family.

Yet the weight of their financial troubles remained, casting a shadow even in their moment of victory. Determined not to let despair seep back in, they made a collective decision: it was time to celebrate.

The families threw themselves into party preparations, eager for a reason to smile. They invited friends from the village, hired a local band, and prepared a feast that would do justice to their Sicilian heritage. In the kitchen, platters piled high with pasta, seafood, and roasted vegetables came together under Marla's expert hands, while others worked outside, stringing up lights and setting up long tables under the stars.

"If these are the last days on the farm," Carlo declared, "then we'll go out with a bang."

As the evening arrived, laughter and music filled the air, and the scent of grilled meats wafted through the warm summer breeze. Guests began to trickle in, dressed in their finest, and the farm slowly transformed into a joyous gathering. The band struck up a lively tune, drawing cheers as the first dancers hit the floor. The clink of glasses, the hum of conversation, and bursts of laughter created an atmosphere of pure joy.

Angela gave her mother a warm hug as they descended the stairs together to join the celebration. Isabella smiled, her eyes glistening. "Thank you, my darling. I'm so proud of you. You've never given up on any of us. You've been the glue holding this family together."

Angela looked into her mother's deep blue eyes, mirroring her own. The golden sunset reflected in their tears, making them both sparkle.

"I've decided to stay here," Isabella continued. "With Roberto. I can't leave now, not after everything. But I'll visit New York often. But this is where I belong now."

Angela hugged her mother tightly. "I know, Mother. You're home here. And someday, I'd like something like this too—a life on the land, caring for animals. Maybe it won't be too long until I join you here."

Isabella kissed her forehead. "You'll always have a home here, Angela. Always."

Hand in hand, they descended into the party, where Michael greeted them at the bottom of the stairs with a grin. "My beautiful mother and sister—can I get you a drink?"

The three of them laughed and joined the merriment. The party was in full swing now, with people dancing, eating, and drinking under the twinkling fairy lights. A traditional Sicilian song started up, and the crowd began to clap, dance and chant in unison. Angela found herself caught up in the excitement, spinning and laughing, until suddenly, she lost her footing and tumbled to the ground.

As she sat there laughing, a strong, familiar hand reached out to help her up. Her breath hitched. That hand—it was unmistakable. Soft yet firm, comforting yet powerful.

She looked up, her heart pounding. Through the haze of party lights and her dizziness, there he was.

"Hello, Ella," Jay said softly, his voice like a balm to her soul. "Need some help?"

Angela gasped, her hands flying to her mouth. "Jay!" He somehow looked more handsome, stronger, his hair longer and his skin glowing with a sun-kissed tan. She stared at him, unable to speak, her mind racing as memories of him flooded her mind. Around them, the party quieted, guests murmuring as they realized what was unfolding.

"Where have you been? What are you doing here?" Angela asked, her voice trembling.

Jay kept his eyes locked on hers, oblivious to the crowd. "I finally called my mom. She told me you'd been looking for me, and then I heard about...everything. The trouble with your family, the poisoning. I came as soon as I could. But I didn't know...I didn't realize you cared enough to look for me." His voice cracked. "I've been lost, Ella. So confused. I just needed space to figure things out."

Just as he reached to pull her into a hug, Jay's expression darkened. His gaze shifted over her shoulder, and his body stiffened.

Angela turned to see where he was looking. Standing a few steps behind her was Michael, smiling warmly at the scene.

Jay's face contorted with hurt and anger. He took a step back, shaking his head. "I've been such a fool. I should've known—when you couldn't find me, you'd run back to him."

"Jay, no! You've got it all wrong—"

"Don't bother." His voice was sharp, cutting through her protests. "I came for you, Ella. I wanted to tell you how sorry I was, to ask for your forgiveness. I realized I made a mistake getting involved in Dan's business. All I ever wanted was you. But the night I came to tell you—late, nearly midnight— I saw you. Outside your apartment. With *him*." Jay angrily pointed at Michael, giving him an icy glare as he spat out his last sentence.

The party guests exchanged awkward glances, whispers spreading as the tension mounted.

Angela's eyes widened. She searched her memory, piecing together the night he described. It hit her like a freight train. That night—Michael had stayed late helping her with an essay.

Jay turned to leave, but Angela darted forward, grabbing his arm.

"Jay, stop," she said, her voice firm yet gentle. She pulled him towards her and cupped his face in her hands, forcing him to meet her gaze. "You've had it wrong this whole time. Michael isn't a threat." Angela paused and started into his hurt eyes. "He's family. He's my brother."

Jay froze, her words sinking in. For a moment, he couldn't breathe. The weight of her revelation collided with the months of doubt and heartache that had consumed him. His mind raced, replaying every sleepless night, every moment he had spent convincing himself that she had moved on, that she had chosen someone else. And all this time, he had been wrong.

His chest tightened as the enormity of his mistake hit him like a tidal wave. He hadn't lost her. He had let her slip away. Angela's words echoed in his head, louder than the music, louder than the whispers of the crowd. *He's my brother.* The walls he had built around himself began to crumble, brick by agonizing brick, as he stared into her tear-filled eyes. Eyes that had never stopped loving him.

Then, without warning, Jay stepped forward and pulled her into a fierce kiss. It wasn't just a kiss—it was an apology, a confession, and a promise all at once. Every ounce of pain, every moment of longing, every unsaid word poured into that single connection.

Angela's hands gripped his shirt as though anchoring herself to him, her tears mixing with his as the world around them seemed to fade. For the first time in months, the emptiness inside Jay dissolved, replaced by the warmth he had been missing since the day he left that café on New Years Eve.

When they finally broke apart, their foreheads rested against each other, their breaths mingling. "I'm sorry, Ella," he whispered hoarsely, his voice raw with emotion. "I've been so stupid. So lost without you."

Angela cupped his face, her thumbs brushing away his tears. "You came back," she whispered, her voice trembling but steady. "That's all that matters."

Jay closed his eyes, holding her close as though afraid he might lose her again if he let go. In that moment, the months of anguish and misunderstanding melted away, leaving only the undeniable truth—they had found their way back to each other.

The crowd erupted in cheers, and Daniel stepped forward to greet his stepson. Isabella and Michael followed, with Angela introducing Jay to her long-lost brother. Jay gave Michael an embarrassed but heartfelt handshake.

"It seems I've got a lot to catch up on," Jay admitted with a sheepish smile.

Angela eventually pulled Jay away from the fuss, her hand tightly gripping his as they slipped through the crowd. The murmurs and cheers faded behind them as they ran down to the beach, where the soft glow of moonlight danced on the gentle waves. Here, where the air was warm and quiet, they could finally be alone.

Angela led him to a spot near the water, where the sand was cool beneath their feet. She turned to face him, her pulse racing, and for a moment, they just stood there, taking each other in. The sound of the ocean filled the space between them as Jay reached out to brush a strand of hair from her face.

"This feels like a dream," he said quietly, his voice laced with awe. "I've thought about this moment a thousand times, but I never thought it would actually happen."

Angela smiled, her fingers grazing his cheek. "You're here, Jay. That's all that matters. You came back to me."

He took her hands in his, holding them against his chest. "I never stopped loving you, Ella. Not for a second. Even when I thought I'd lost you, even when I tried to convince myself it was over, you were always there—here." He placed her hand over his heart.

Tears pricked at her eyes again, but they were different this time. They weren't tears of sadness or frustration—they were tears of relief, of joy. "I've missed you so much," she whispered. "Everything feels right now that you're here."

Jay smiled, his golden-brown skin glowing softly in the moonlight. "I'll never leave again. I promise."

They sat down together in the sand, leaning against each other as the waves lapped gently at the shore. Angela rested her head on his shoulder, and Jay wrapped an arm around her, pulling her close. For a while, neither of them spoke—they didn't need to.

The world around them seemed to fade away, leaving only the sound of the sea and the rhythm of their hearts beating in unison. Jay ran his fingers through her hair, and Angela traced little patterns on his arm, both of them soaking in the comfort and love they had longed for.

As the night stretched on, Angela tilted her head up to look at him. "Jay," she said softly, her voice carrying the weight of all the emotions she'd been holding back, "Where have you been all this time? What have you been doing?" Angela asked softly, her voice tinged with hesitation. She paused, searching his face. "Was there ever anyone else?"

Jay chuckled quietly, his expression tender as he leaned in to kiss her, his touch reassuring. "Ella, there has only ever been you. You've consumed my thoughts for so long now."

He exhaled deeply, as though recounting the weight of his journey. "I traveled quickly through Italy, hardly stopping anywhere. No place felt right, no place could ease the restless feeling inside me. I was searching for something—anything—that could bring me peace. But nothing soothed my soul.

Then, just outside Naples, I stumbled upon this small, beautiful town. The people there were kind, welcoming, and wise. They listened without judgment, and one local man even offered me a job at his bar to help distract me. I started teaching English to the locals, and for a while, I felt a flicker of relief, like I could finally breathe again.

But then I finally called my mom. That's when she told me you'd come looking for me—that you were in Sicily with your parents trying to save the farm. The moment I heard that, I knew I couldn't stay away. I had to come here. I had to be there for you."

Angela smiled, her eyes brimming with emotion as she held his hands tighter. "I'm so glad you did." Angela turned around to look him straight into the eyes. "Jay, promise me we'll always find our way back to each other, no matter what."

He kissed her forehead, then her lips, his voice steady as he replied. "I promise, Ella. Always."

And as they sat there under the stars, tangled together and surrounded by the endless horizon, Angela knew this was where she belonged. With him, everything felt possible again.

37

The next morning, Angela woke to the sound of frantic screams echoing through the farmhouse. Her heart skipped a beat as she sat up, still groggy from the late night of celebrations. The two families had stayed together in the main house, too tired to make the trip back to the other house or Roberto's after the festivities. She quickly realized the screams belonged to Bianca.

"It's midday! Everyone, wake up and come downstairs! I need to talk to you all!" Bianca's voice was breathless, urgent but filled with excitement.

One by one, the family stumbled into the dining room, still rubbing the sleep from their eyes. Bianca stood in the center of the room, practically vibrating with energy, while

Daniel hovered beside her, his expression unreadable but calm.

Bianca's grin was so wide it looked as though she might burst. "So, Father and I were called into town this morning for an urgent meeting with the CEO of Gruppo di Vita." She paused for dramatic effect, her chest rising and falling as she tried to contain herself. "And you'll never guess what happened."

The room was silent, the family exchanging confused glances.

"Well, they've offered to settle out of court!" Bianca's voice pitched higher with excitement, but the statement took a second to sink in.

Maria gasped. "Settle? What does that mean?" she asked, her hands clutching Isabella's arm.

Daniel stepped in, his tone steady and serious, though his eyes gleamed with triumph. "They're prepared to pay a substantial settlement to make this scandal disappear. If we agree, they'll leave the farm alone—no more interference, no more threats."

"How much?" Isabella asked, standing slowly from her chair. Her voice was calm, but the weight of the question made the air feel charged.

Daniel glanced at Bianca, allowing her to deliver the news. Bianca didn't hesitate—she practically screamed. "Two million dollars! They're offering two million!"

The room erupted. Franco and Vincenzo leaped out of their chairs, fists in the air, while Caterina clasped her hands to her chest, falling to her knees and crying out in gratitude. Maria hugged Isabella tightly, tears streaming down her face.

"Thank you, Daniel, thank you, Bianca," Maria sobbed. "You have saved us. This is more than enough to save the farm and secure the future of our family for generations."

Bianca beamed as Daniel raised his hands to quiet the chaos. "This wasn't just Bianca and me. This was a team effort. Every single one of us played a part in making this happen. We did this together."

The family all joined together, hugging and jumping for joy as they could finally feel a deep relief after the months of worry and stress this ordeal had caused them.

Later that afternoon, everyone gathered for a celebratory lunch at the long dining table. The atmosphere was electric with relief and joy. Glasses clinked together, and laughter echoed through the room. Jay sat beside Angela, his hand entwined tightly with hers, the connection between them obvious for all to see.

As they shared stories and soaked in the warmth of the moment, Jay leaned in close to Angela, his voice low and intimate. "So, Ella... what now? Are you thinking what I'm thinking?"

Angela tilted her head, a curious smile playing on her lips. "What are you thinking, Jay?"

He squeezed her hand. "We finish school, then come back to Sicily. Make a life here, like we always dreamed. You've always wanted to be part of something like this—living on the land, surrounded by animals, with a family like this. I could even teach English to the locals. What do you say?"

Angela's smile widened, her eyes shining with emotion. In that moment, she felt like everything had fallen into place.

"You read my mind. Mother and I had talked about this yesterday. That sounds like bliss to me."

Before Jay could respond, the sound of a glass clinking silenced the table. Everyone turned to see Roberto standing at the head, his face flushed and his hands trembling slightly as he gestured for quiet.

"Thank you," he began, his voice wavering. "Thank you, everyone, from the bottom of my heart. We are all here today as two families, brought together under the most unusual and challenging circumstances. And yet, through it all, we've supported one another. We've laughed, cried, and fought like any family does. But I have to say... I've never felt more connected to all of you than I do right now."

The room fell silent, the weight of his words sinking in.

"For most of my life, the Lombardos and the Veronas have shared a deep connection. We've been there for each other through thick and thin. And though we are not tied by blood, we've always been like family. But today..." He paused, taking a deep breath. "Today, I'd like to change that."

Gasps rippled through the room as Roberto stepped away from his chair and walked toward Isabella, his steps deliberate and his expression soft with emotion. Slowly, he lowered himself onto one knee, reaching for her hand.

The table collectively held their breath, hands covering mouths as tears welled in Angela's eyes. Her mother's face was a mixture of shock and joy.

"My beautiful Isabella," Roberto began, his voice thick with emotion. "I have waited a lifetime for this moment, and I do not regret a second of it. You have been my rock, my heart, my everything. Will you do me the honor of becoming my wife? Will you finally make our families one, once and for all?"

Isabella's hands flew to her mouth as tears spilled down her cheeks. Without hesitation, she threw her arms around him and shouted, "Yes! Yes, Roberto, I will marry you!"

The room erupted in applause and cheers, laughter and tears blending together as the two embraced. Jay wrapped his arms around Angela, pulling her close as the celebration continued.

Angela squeezed him, love bloomed within her as she was filled with gratitude. Looking at her mother's joy, Roberto's love, and the family united around the table, she knew this was the start of something new—not just for her mother, but for all of them.

Jay kissed the top of her head, whispering, "This is just the beginning, Ella. The best is yet to come."

Angela smiled, leaning into him as the cheers and laughter of her family filled the air around them. A wave of relief swept over her, loosening the tension she had carried for so long. She could suddenly breath after months of worry and unease. Life wasn't perfect—she knew it never would be. Plans unraveled, and challenges arose, but deep down, she understood she would always find her way through. And in that very moment, with Jay by her side once more, everything felt beautifully, wonderfully and perfectly right.

Printed in Dunstable, United Kingdom

74719149R00129